A MAN FOR ALL
BY ROBERT

MACMILLAN MASTER GUIDES

General Editor: James Gibson

Published:
JANE AUSTEN: **EMMA** Norman Page
ROBERT BOLT: **A MAN FOR ALL SEASONS** Leonard Smith
EMILY BRONTË: **WUTHERING HEIGHTS** Hilda D. Spear
GEOFFREY CHAUCER: **THE PROLOGUE TO THE CANTERBURY TALES** Nigel Thomas and Richard Swan
CHARLES DICKENS: **GREAT EXPECTATIONS** Dennis Butts
GEORGE ELIOT: **SILAS MARNER** Graham Handley
GEORGE ORWELL: **ANIMAL FARM** Jean Armstrong
WILLIAM SHAKESPEARE: **MACBETH** David Elloway
A MIDSUMMER NIGHT'S DREAM Kenneth Pickering
ROMEO AND JULIET Helen Morris

Forthcoming:
JANE AUSTEN: **MANSFIELD PARK** Richard Wirdnam
PRIDE AND PREJUDICE Raymond Wilson
CHARLES DICKENS: **HARD TIMES** Norman Page
GEORGE ELIOT: **MIDDLEMARCH** Graham Handley
T. S. ELIOT: **MURDER IN THE CATHEDRAL** Paul Lapworth
OLIVER GOLDSMITH: **SHE STOOPS TO CONQUER** Paul Ranger
THOMAS HARDY: **FAR FROM THE MADDING CROWD** Colin Temblett-Wood
TESS OF THE D'URBERVILLES James Gibson
CHRISTOPHER MARLOWE: **DR FAUSTUS** David Male
THE METAPHYSICAL POETS Joan van Emden
WILLIAM SHAKESPEARE: **HAMLET** Jean Brooks
TWELFTH NIGHT Edward Leeson
THE WINTER'S TALE Diana Devlin
GEORGE BERNARD SHAW: **ST JOAN** Leonee Ormond
R. B. SHERIDAN: **THE RIVALS** Jeremy Rowe

Also published by Macmillan

MACMILLAN MASTER SERIES

Mastering English Literature R. Gill
Mastering English Language S. H. Burton
Mastering English Grammar S. H. Burton

MACMILLAN MASTER GUIDES

A MAN FOR ALL SEASONS

BY ROBERT BOLT

LEONARD SMITH

MACMILLAN

First edition 1985

Published by
MACMILLAN EDUCATION LTD
Houndmills, Basingstoke, Hampshire RG21 2XS
and London
Companies and representatives
throughout the world

Printed in Hong Kong

British Library Cataloguing in Publication Data
Smith, Leonard
A man for all seasons by Robert Bolt.—
(Macmillan master guides)
1.   Bolt, Robert. Man for all seasons
1.   Title
822' PR.914   PR6003.0474Z/
ISBN 0-333-37435-5
ISBN 0-333-39297-3   export

CONTENTS

GENERAL EDITOR'S PREFACE

The aim of the Macmillan Master Guides is to help you to appreciate the book you are studying by providing information about it and by suggesting ways of reading and thinking about it which will lead to a fuller understanding. The section on the writer's life and background has been designed to illustrate those aspects of the writer's life which have influenced the work, and to place it in its personal and literary context. The summaries and critical commentary are of special importance in that each brief summary of the action is followed by an examination of the significant critical points. The space which might have been given to repetitive explanatory notes has been devoted to a detailed analysis of the kind of passage which might confront you in an examination. Literary criticism is concerned with both the broader aspects of the work being studied and with its detail. The ideas which meet us in reading a great work of literature, and their relevance to us today, are an essential part of our study, and our Guides look at the thought of their subject in some detail. But just as essential is the craft with which the writer has constructed his work of art, and this is considered under several technical headings – characterisation, language, style and stagecraft.

The authors of these Guides are all teachers and writers of wide experience, and they have chosen to write about books they admire and know well in the belief that they can communicate their admiration to you. But you yourself must read and know intimately the book you are studying. No one can do that for you. You should see this book as a lamppost. Use it to shed light, not to lean against. If you know your text and know what it is saying about life, and how it says it, then you will enjoy it, and there is no better way of passing an examination in literature.

JAMES GIBSON

ACKNOWLEDGEMENTS

The editor and publishers wish to thank the following who have kindly given permission for the use of copyright material: Basil Blackwell Limited for an extract from *Thomas More, History and Providence* by Alistair Fox; Jonathan Cape Ltd on behalf of the Executors of the R. W. Chambers Estate for an extract from *Thomas More*; Heinemann Educational Books Ltd for extracts from *Vivat, Vivat Regina!* by Robert Bolt; Heinemann Educational Books Ltd and Random House Inc. for extracts from *A Man for All Seasons* by Robert Bolt; Margaret Ramsey Ltd on behalf of Robert Bolt for an extract from the radio play *A Man for All Seasons*.

Cover illustration: *Portrait of Sir Thomas More*, after Holbein, courtesy of the National Portrait Gallery.

1 INTRODUCTION

When studying *A Man for All Seasons* you must constantly keep in mind that it is a work of art written for performance on the stage. If you are not lucky enough to see a performance, you must imagine how it would appear on a stage. The dramatic impact of the play depends not only on the words spoken by the actors, but also on the effect of costumes, stage properties, sounds on and off stage, lighting, and many other theatrical devices, including the reactions of the audience.

Before Robert Bolt wrote the stage version of *A Man for All Seasons*, he had been involved in the production of his first successful stage play, *Flowering Cherry*, so he knew all the possibilities provided by the modern professional theatre, and he used them extensively in this play. One reason for the world-wide success of this play is that it is so dramatically effective in the theatre; not only the producer and actors, but also the costume designers, the 'props' men, the sound effects and lighting engineers, all have a rewarding time when this play is staged, and this co-operative creative achievement makes its impact on the audience.

So don't study *A Man for All Seasons* as you would a novel, short story or poem. You must read not only the words spoken by the characters, but also imagine how they would be delivered on the stage; you must read all the stage directions carefully, and imagine what effect they would have, not only the visual effects of costumes, props, changes of scene and the use of lighting, but also the sounds.

It is possible that you have seen the film of *A Man for All Seasons*, or a video of the film, and not the stage production. Although the script for the film was written by Bolt himself, and he was closely involved in its production, the film is in many ways different from the play. The central themes, and many of the words spoken by the characters are the same; but many of the devices by which Bolt achieves his impact on the audience are quite different. When he came to write the scenario for the film, Bolt had worked closely with the producer, David Lean, on the production of the film *Lawrence of Arabia*, for which he wrote the script. He quickly realised that plays and films work in different ways. For example, with a film there is no interaction between the audience and the actors; so, in the film, Bolt leaves out the character of the Common Man, who, on the stage, is the chief link between the audience and the action on the stage. In the play, the importance of water and the river can be suggested only by imagery, and to a lesser extent, by lighting effects; in the film it was possible to have scenes actually shot on the river, with King Henry jumping into the mud. So, although it is valuable to see such a splendid film, you must remember that it is not the same as the play. And it is the play that you must study - and, I hope, enjoy.

2 ROBERT BOLT AND THE BACKGROUND TO THE PLAY

2.1 FROM METHODIST TO COMMUNIST

Robert Oxton Bolt was born in Manchester in 1924. His father kept a small furniture shop. His family were Methodists and he had to go to chapel twice every Sunday until he was sixteen. Then, given the choice, he never went again. But although he has said it is his misfortune to have no religion, he adds: 'But the fact remains that the groundswell of my thought only makes sense on the assumption that there is Somebody to whom I am responsible' (Ronald Hayman, *Robert Bolt*, page 15).

In his interview in 1969 with Ronald Hayman about his life, he said his childhood was not a happy one, and he was always bottom of the class. But he was always very good at English, and wrote stories and poems from an early age.

At sixteen he went to work in an insurance office, an experience he hated, and which later provided some material for the character of Jim Cherry in his second stage play, *Flowering Cherry*. However, given the chance to go to Manchester University, he passed three A Levels by studying in the evenings for just five weeks. This was during the Second World War, in 1942. University opened out a much wider social life for him, with interests in music and politics, and he became a Marxist and joined the Communist Party.

This was a fairly usual experience for young people at that time who were, as Bolt said of himself, 'naturally constituted to be religious', but yet rejected the Church in any form. The First World War (1914–18), when millions of people had been killed, caused many people to question the social regimes that could lead to such slaughter; and the Russian Revolution of 1917 was seen by many as an alternative way of organising society. The slump and mass unemployment that followed the war in the 1920s and 30s caused many people to question the morality of capitalism. Then the rise of Fascism in Italy and Germany in the 1930s, and the overthrow of democracy in Spain during the Spanish Civil War (1936–39), caused many other intellectuals in Europe and America to look towards Communism as offering a political alternative. News of the purges in Stalinist Russia did come through to the West, but for many, this did not dim the *ideal* of Communism. When Hitler's Germany attacked the Soviet Union in 1942, and Russia became the ally of the Western democracies, many Western Marxists felt that their faith was vindicated.

After one year at university, Bolt went into the Royal Air Force as a cadet-pilot, and went to South Africa for his flying training. He was later, through air-sickness, taken off flying training, and had to wait three months in Cape Town for a troopship back to England. This was a joyous time for Bolt. He said it showed him the possibility of enjoying life without hurting anybody. He had never been abroad before, and found the Cape Peninsula 'more beautiful than anything I've seen in the Mediterranean'. Furthermore, after the drabness of war-time life in England, there was a flourishing theatrical life in Cape Town, with several people, such as the choreographer John Cranko, who later made international reputations.

From this 'wine and peaches and all kinds of harmless junketings', as he called it, he was brought back to England in the dead of winter, and noticed for the first time, just how ugly the slums and factories of industrial Manchester were. He was then drafted into the army, and spent some time in West Africa as an officer, before returning to Manchester University in 1947 for three years to take an honours degree in History.

2.2 REJECTION OF COMMUNISM

All this time Bolt had remained a Communist, although this was supposed to be illegal for any member of the Forces. But back at university, and beginning to enjoy a new-found freedom of life and thought, Bolt found he could no longer go along with the 'Party line', so, after five years as a member, he left the Communist Party. For a while, he has said, he flirted with the ideas of such people as the Jewish philosopher Martin Buber (1878–1965), and Zen and Lao-Tse-Taoism, but, in the end, he came to the conclusion that 'philosophically and spiritually you are stuck with yourself and any good you achieve you will achieve in yourself and any evil you suffer you will suffer in yourself' (Hayman, page 7).

In his interview with Hayman, Bolt mentions his elder brother, who, in contrast to himself, was very successful at school. And it was his brother who first showed promise as a writer, contributing to intellectual magazines, where his name, S. F. Bolt, is to be found with those of such writers as the novelist George Orwell and the French philosopher Jean-Paul Sartre. In one of these he reviewed Martin Buber's *Between Man and Man*, in which he writes: 'Acknowledgement of a responsibility which cannot be delegated is undoubtedly the first essential for any form of adult life. . .' ('Politics and Letters', vol. I, Nos 2 & 3, 1974). Many years later, Robert Bolt acknowledged that 'Buber had an effect on the way I thought', and went on to say: 'What I was trying to say in the preface to *A Man for All Seasons* was not just that it's the individual that counts but that the individual is all there *is*.'

So, philosophically – and religiously, although not identified with any recognised religion – Bolt was led from a Methodist background, by way of Communism and its rejection, through a flirtation with Christian, Jewish and Eastern mystics, to a belief in the obligations and responsibilities of the individual, guided by his conscience, because that is 'all there *is*'. This is one reason why he was attracted towards Sir Thomas More.

2.3 CONFLICT WITH THE STATE OVER THE BOMB

More was a sympathetic hero because during the 1950s Bolt found himself in conflict with what the State, that is, the British Government, was doing with the development, testing and stockpiling of hydrogen bombs. Bolt could not support the blatant anti-Russian hysteria which was being used to justify the arms race once again, and particularly The Atom Bomb, which, because of its vast destructive power, many saw as intrinsically evil, and not to be used either in fact, or as a 'deterrent'. This matter so touched Bolt's conscience that after he had written *A Man for All Seasons*, he agreed to join the Committee of One Hundred, a group of writers and intellectuals organised by the philosopher Bertrand Russell, who agreed to break the law to call attention to the dangers of nuclear war. This was an extremely painful decision for Bolt, because he was naturally, and by intellectual conviction, a law-abiding citizen. As he said to Hayman: 'I have respect for the law because I think that the human being is a potentially chaotic and destructive creature and society and the law are infinitely valuable.' This is another reason why Sir Thomas More attracted Bolt: More believed in the sanctity of 'the thickets of the law'.

However, because of his depth of feeling over The Bomb, Bolt was willing to join the protests, which took the form of 'civil disobedience'. He refused to be 'bound over to keep the peace' and was sent to prison. Bolt says he was 'deeply shocked' by this experience – although 'the rough warders and tin plates and jerry in the cell' were nothing when compared with what More experienced in the Tower of London. But Bolt, too, came under similar pressures to those experienced by More. Family and friends were mostly supportive of his 'stand'; but he was at this time involved in his first film script, *Lawrence of Arabia* (1962), which was being shot while he wrote it, and the whole production was held up. The producer, Sam Spiegel, went to the prison and put pressure on Bolt to come out; Spiegel pointed out that the film crew would be out of work and thousands of dollars lost. It was, of course, extremely ironic that so soon after writing about More and the pressures that he had to endure, Bolt found himself in the same position. Like Arthur Miller in his *The Crucible* (see page 58) Bolt had anticipated his own fate. But, unlike the hero of his play, Bolt gave way. In his own words: 'I bound myself over and came out, and bitterly and instantly regretted it... Although there were very good reasons why I should, I knew that ultimately I should *not* have come out and it was simply because Sam had built up the pressure to such an extent that I couldn't hold out. For about six months afterwards I found it very hard to look at myself in the mirror' (Hayman, page 13).

Some critics have complained that Bolt's plays are not emotionally involved with his own experience. From this very short survey, it can be seen that *A Man for All Seasons* was most intimately bound up with Bolt's intellectual, moral and emotional life during the 1950s. Through this play Bolt was living out, in the person of Sir Thomas More, many of the difficult decisions and pressures that he knew he would have to go through if he were to be true to his conscience. And that he gave in, where More had been willing to face death, was one reason why he had found it difficult to look at himself in the mirror. He had 'opened his fingers' at the crucial moment. His play, however, must have given solace to many other people, all over the world, who have found their conscience at variance with the demands of the state.

2.4 DEVELOPMENT AS PLAYWRIGHT

When Bolt wrote *A Man for All Seasons* he was not only emotionally involved; he was also technically ready. After he had left university, he went, rather romantically, to teach at the village school at Topsham in Devon. It was at this school that Bolt was asked to write a nativity play for the children to perform. He has said that he knew after writing just six lines of dialogue that this was what he wanted to do with his life. By this time he was married with a child.

He followed the nativity play with a radio play called *The Master*, first broadcast in February, 1953, and soon after Bolt went to teach at Millfield School, the most expensive independent school in England, an odd choice for someone who had been a Communist. But teaching at Millfield left Bolt time to write a number of radio plays. Bolt and his wife, and daughter and son who was born soon after they moved to Somerset, lived in a thatched fourteenth-century cottage with no running water, in the village of Butleigh, not far from the mystical centre of Glastonbury. This was a very productive time for Bolt. Fields full of dandelion flowers on the way to school were the starting point for a radio play, *The Last of the Wine* (1956), on an anti-nuclear theme; a poster on a farm building advertising an auction for fifty pigs, resulted in a comedy of that name; visits to buy vegetables at the local 'big house' with its dilapidated greenhouses, gave rise to a children's play called *The Banana Tree*.

More's *Utopia* was one of the set books on the exam syllabus at this time, and it was natural that Bolt, with his historical background, should teach this book. This was another of the strands that led him to write a play about the extraordinary man who wrote *Utopia*.

Given the favourable circumstances at Millfield, Bolt was an excellent teacher. He has said that 'if you can arouse a child's desire to learn, you are not half-way home, you're four-fifths of the way home', and he could always make his pupils want to learn by making the subject interesting, and by showing that it was alive and important to them. He has related the technique of good teaching to that of the playwright – arousing the audience's desire to learn about the characters on the stage, and be told what happens to them.

So a combination of political, personal and technical circumstances all came together at the same time when Bolt was ready to write the first radio version of what was to become his most popular play. Spurred on by this success, he adapted it for television, in which he began to explore some of the visual imagery and symbolism used in the later stage play, and then write his first plays for the stage. The first of these, *The Critic and the Heart*, was performed at the Oxford Playhouse in April, 1957. In November of the same year, *Flowering Cherry* was performed at the Haymarket in London, with Sir Ralph Richardson and Celia Johnson. It was a great success and ran for over a year. This enabled Bolt to give up teaching and concentrate on writing, and it also gave him an insight into the technical possibilities of the modern stage, which he embraced enthusiastically. These he was to use in the stage version of *A Man for All Seasons* which he wrote in the late 1950s.

Meanwhile, the political situation had intensified, and Bolt's own attitude towards it had clarified. When he came to write the stage version of his play, which was his third attempt at the same topic, he was both personally and technically in exactly the right state of commitment and excitement to write it. This no doubt accounts, to a large extent, for both the technical accomplishment of the play with its intricate patterning, and for its emotional intensity.

2.5 SUBSEQUENT WORK

After *A Man for All Seasons* Bolt wrote several other plays: *The Tiger and the Horse*, first performed in 1960; *Gentle Jack*, 1963; a children's play, *The Thwarting of Baron Bolligrew*, 1965; *Vivat! Vivat Regina!*, 1970; and *State of Revolution*, first performed at the National Theatre, London, in 1977. None of these has had, as yet, the success of *A Man for All Seasons*, although the children's play has been revived many times.

After the success of *A Man for All Seasons*, much of Bolt's creative energy went into writing film scripts, where he worked with the director David Lean on *Lawrence of Arabia* (1962), *Doctor Zhivago* (1964), *Ryan's Daughter* (1970), and the film of *A Man for All Seasons* (1967) which has taken it to an even wider audience. It is now the film version, and not the play as originally written, that is still sometimes seen on television. He has also directed his own film, *Lady Caroline Lamb* (1972) which he wrote for his second wife, the actress Sarah Miles. *The Bounty* (1984) is his latest film.

3 SUMMARY AND CRITICAL COMMENTARY

PLOT SYNOPSIS

Henry VIII, King of England in the sixteenth century, wanted a male heir. England was then a Catholic country, so he obtained a special dispensation from the Pope to marry his brother's widow, Catherine. But when Catherine produced no male child, Henry wanted to divorce her and marry Anne Boleyn. Divorce was forbidden by the Catholic Church, but Henry, not to be outdone, found evidence in the Bible that his marriage to Catherine had been sinful: so the Pope, by forbidding the divorce, was keeping Henry in a state of sin. Henry, therefore, had the Act of Succession passed in Parliament, denied the Pope's authority, and established the Church of England.

Because of Henry's power, most of his advisers and noblemen agreed with him. However, the most brilliant, repected and popular of his councillors, whom he had made Chancellor after Cardinal Wolsey had been charged with treason, refused to go with him. This was Sir Thomas More. He was a devout Christian, and his conscience would not allow him to deny the authority of the Pope. To do so would be to deny himself as a human being. So when the bishops agreed with Henry's actions, More resigned the Chancellorship.

To deny the Act of Succession was treasonable; but More, as a lawyer, knew that 'silence means consent', so he refused to give his opinion to anyone. No threats, not even imprisonment, would make him budge. Neither would entreaties from his friend, the Duke of Norfolk, nor from his wife Alice, daughter Margaret and son-in-law Roper.

But Henry was not to be denied. He made Thomas Cromwell Chancellor, and when *his* threats would not break More's resolve, he made Richard Rich perjure himself by saying he had heard More deny the Act. Only then did More, before he was beheaded, speak his mind. He had been true to himself to the end.

Act 1, Prologue

Summary
The Common Man tells the audience about the time and place of the play, and introduces some of the characters.

Commentary
When people enter a theatre and take their seats, they do so as individuals; Bolt wants to mould them into an audience, and he does this by making them laugh. Laughter brings individuals together, making them react in unison. The black tights that the Common Man wears not only 'delineate his pot-bellied figure', but also his genitals, emphasised by the 'single spot which descends vertically'. This makes many people in the audience feel uncomfortable, which Bolt also wants – the experience of the play is not going to be 'comfortable'. But when the Common Man says 'Oh, if they'd let me come on naked, I could have shown you something of my own', the joke releases the embarrassment in laughter. The audience is now united.

But more than this has happened. The play has started by making the audience aware that each of us is a naked, sinful creature, 'this poor, bare, forked animal' as Shakespeare says in *King Lear*. How can we attempt to achieve human dignity from such unpromising material? The Common Man doesn't try to attempt it. 'Something I've forgotton. . .Old Adam's muffled up' implies he is impotent, sexually and morally, so he is prepared to play any part that comes easily to him (as do most 'common' men and women). As his first performance, he takes on the part of the Household Steward of Sir Thomas More to introduce a man who *will* reveal that it is possible to give 'a nearly faultless. . .performance as a human being', as Bolt himself commented in his interviews about the play with Ronald Hayman.

This Prologue, largely ignored by most commentators, deserves close and detailed study for its richness of suggestions, puns, implications and symbolism, all of which are relevant to the theme of the play. The audience has been immediately 'engaged' and is then taken into the play by the Common Man when he himself enters the action.

The transition from Prologue to the first scene begins when the *'lights come up swiftly on set'*, showing a table in More's house furnished for dinner. But before the new scene begins, the Common Man explains his 'proposition': although the play is set in the sixteenth century, its action is just as relevant for the twentieth century, because all centuries are 'the Century of the Common Man'. Then, by his actions, he shows himself capable of corruption and petty pilfering by drinking his master's wine, and although this pilfering is petty, it is symbolically of major importance.

The stagecraft of this transition scene should be studied carefully. The play on the words 'All right' as an exclamation, to 'All right' as comment on the wine, is a clever pun; and the breaks in action when the steward 'regards the jug respectfully and drinks again', involve the members of the audience. They cannot stop themselves from laughing, and so partake of his actions, showing themselves to be easily corruptible: they would have done the same in his position. Meanwhile, the silver goblet, which later in the play is going to show that More is incorruptible, has already been placed on the table by the Common Man in his part as 'Steward'.

L. C. Knights says in *An Approach to Hamlet*: 'Right at the start of each of his tragedies, Shakespeare establishes the "atmosphere" – something that is not just a vaguely effective background but an integral part of the play's structure of meaning.' Bolt has done the same in this short Prologue.

Act 1, scene 1

Summary
Sir Thomas More, his wife Alice and daughter Margaret are introduced, also Richard Rich and the Duke of Norfolk. Rich and More discuss a man's 'price'; Norfolk and Alice argue about a falcon. The theme of the motive for action is introduced. Rich is offered the silver goblet by More, who tries to persuade him to be a teacher. Although it is eleven o'clock at night, More is summoned to meet Wolsey on the King's business.

Commentary
When More asks the Steward if the wine is good, and the Steward says he doesn't know, More's reply in blessing him shows that he knows that this, and every other 'common man', is capable of pilfering and telling lies about it.

Rich's comment that every man has his 'price' introduces the theme of how a man's 'worth' can be measured. Rich believes that every man can be corrupted if offered the right temptation. When he suggests that some men can be bought by 'suffering', More is 'interested' because he thinks that Rich means the temptation of martyrdom. Here, as elsewhere in this play, Bolt is reflecting themes to be found in T. S. Eliot's play *Murder in the Cathedral*. In that play the Fourth Tempter whom Thomas Becket had 'not expected', but who tells him what he 'already knows', says: 'Seek the way of martyrdom, make yourself the lowest/On earth, to be high in heaven.' Much of the dialogue between Becket and the four Tempters is relevant to the themes of Bolt's play. Even the 'falcon' appears as a 'hawk', both symbolising, among other things, the action of the King. But all Rich had meant was that a man can be 'bought' by torturing him (either physically or mentally) and then offering to stop the torture.

More realises, from the ideas that Rich is expounding, that he had been reading Machiavelli's *The Prince*. Written in Italy in 1513, *The Prince* was on the proscribed list in England until well into the seventeenth century, but its impact on sixteenth-century European political thinking was as widespread and potent as another banned book, Karl Marx's *Communist Manifesto* (1847) was to be in the nineteenth and twentieth centuries. Machiavelli subordinated morality to political expediency, the individual to the state. This leads to a belief that 'the ends justify the means', which is completely contrary to Bolt's morality as explored in this play, and also in a later play, *State of Revolution*.

More is interested to learn that it is Cromwell who had directed Rich's reading, and he realises that if Rich stays in politics he will be easily corrupted, and a dangerous man (as, indeed, he proves to be to More); so More advises him to keep out of danger by leading a quiet life as a teacher. Rich however, wants power, he wants to be 'used'. This word introduces another theme, often explored by Shakespeare in his plays. No person should 'use' another person. Rich's contemptible nature is shown by his wanting to be 'used' by a man of power as a step on the ladder to gain power himself. (By contrast, More's high office was 'inflicted' on him.) Rich's base nature is also shown by his willingness to accept the silver goblet even though it was 'contaminated'.

When the Duke of Norfolk and Alice enter, the argument about the falcon, although it introduces some light relief after the rather 'grim' exchange between More and Rich, is by no means irrelevant to the central theme of the play. In one way, the falcon is a symbol for More himself, who did what he had to do, without 'caring' what would happen to him. But More is even more 'tremendous' than the falcon because he is fully aware of what he is doing, and doesn't do it instinctively. His words 'there *are* such birds' could be transposed to 'there *are* such men'.

But, in another way, More is also the victim of the falcon, which is also a symbol for the King, who stoops (in the technical sense of falconry – 'it was a royal stoop') blindly but unerringly on his victim, More, who, unlike the heron, does not take evasive action and does not 'get home to his chicks'. Norfolk would have thought More's action 'very discreditable' if he had taken evasive action when threatened by death. Everybody (apart from Rich) expresses surprised horror when Norfolk gives the news that Cromwell had become Cardinal Wolsey's secretary, and More realises that Rich will not need his help if he has 'friends' in high places.

The transition to the next scene begins when the Steward hands More a letter from the Cardinal. The late hour of the summons introduces an element of anxiety: why should More be summoned so late at night?

The Steward's words to the audience about More's generosity and 'there must be something that he wants to keep' forewarns the audience that there is going to be something More will not give away. The Common Man, because he can stand outside the action of the play, both in time and space, knows what is going to happen to More, and so his comments are not only on what *is* happening, but also hint at what is going to happen, alerting the audience's expectation.

The Prologue and first scene need particularly careful study, because in them Bolt establishes, both directly and by implication, the main themes of the play, and hints at the coming events that cast their shadow before them. Most of the main characters have also been introduced and established either in person or by being talked about. The general atmosphere of the play – the playful, honest informality of More's home life contrasted with the unscrupulous, suspicious background of public life – has also been established.

Act 2, scene 2

Summary
Wolsey attempts to make More agree to support the King's divorce, but More refuses to acquiesce.

Commentary
Wolsey's boorish bad manners are immediately established by his continuing to sit and write while More is kept waiting. The lie he tells about the time, although it is treated as a joke by the audience when the clock strikes one, is nevertheless significant: if you tell lies about small things, it is easy to tell lies about big things.

Wolsey's intention of ignoring the Council, a body of influential states-men and lawyers who advised the King, shows his arrogant high-handedness; More's advice that the dispatch should be shown to the Council shows his respect for established procedures. It is easier to make Machiavellian decisions than to go through the more laborious processes of consultation. Or, in twentieth-century terms, democracy is more difficult than dictatorship. The phrase 'moral squint' shows Wolsey's superficial contempt for More's integrity. Deep down, he probably admired him for just this quality. More, of course, is by no means a 'plodder'; he knows exactly what Wolsey wants, but both his legal training, and his politeness, stop him from anticipating anything.

The introduction of the King into the scene with the off-stage 'single trumpet call, distant, frosty and clear' is a clever piece of stagecraft because it brings the presence of the King immediately into the room, and when Wolsey and More look out of the window, the audience, in imagination, looks out with them, and so becomes involved in the King's 'playing in the muck'.

Wolsey's 'Thomas, we're alone' is another lie. There is a state informer hidden somewhere in the room, listening to every word. (Nowadays there might be a bugging device to record the conversation.) Wolsey's question which is spoken 'deliberately loud', to make the informer alert, is an attempt to provoke More into some treasonable indiscretion that could be used against him. Wolsey's lack of genuine religious feeling, although he is a Cardinal, is shown by his cynical dismissal of More's 'steady' comment that he prays daily for the birth of a son for the King. The candle that Wolsey holds up to More's face is another ambiguous symbol; in one way it stands for 'light', reasonableness and peace (which is why Wolsey later extinguishes it, and then More symbolically relights it at the end of the scene); but the candle can also be painful fire, as when, at the very end of the act, Cromwell holds Rich's hand in the candle flame.

The crux of this scene, and the clearest statement so far of the main theme of the play, comes towards the end: the clash between affairs of state and a person's private conscience. To Wolsey, from expediency, the state comes first: but More's 'Well. . .I believe, when statesmen forsake their own private conscience for the sake of their public duties. . .they lead their country by a short route to chaos' is spoken directly at the modern audience.

Throughout this scene there is a grim undercurrent of humour. Both men are extremely intelligent and, in some ways, they respect each other. Wolsey tries by appeals, reasoning and threats to win More's approval for the divorce; but More will not commit himself.

Act 1, scene 3

Summary
After leaving Wolsey, More meets Cromwell and then Chapuys.

Commentary

The lighting effect of the transition from the previous scene brings the reflection of moonlit water on to the stage. (The symbolism of water in this play is fully discussed in the section on Imagery, on page 72). The Common Man now takes on the part of a Boatman, but any attempt at realism is dismissed by an oar and a bundle of clothing being lowered from above. This tells the audience that what it is seeing is not reality, but a symbolic representation.

The stage directions *pleasantly* and *comfortably* should be noted. The Boatman is almost unconsciously hypocritical, being pleasant and familiar – but he is doing this in an attempt to exploit More for his own gain. That Cromwell appears so late at night and in such dark circumstances, immediately stamps him as a sinister character. Was it *he* who had been listening to the conversation between Wolsey and More in the previous scene? If so, Wolsey's words 'allow for an enemy here' take on a new significance. But then, why does Cromwell now show himself to More? That he insists on the Boatman keeping to the 'fixed' fares is a cruel pun: Cromwell would 'fix' anything for his own benefit. His exaggerated pleasure on seeing More, and his insincere words 'one of your *multitudinous* admirers' demonstrate his hypocritical nature. His appearance against the dark background of the stage is felt as a physical threat to More. But More is still politely non-committal.

Then the appearance of Chapuys and his attendant further emphasises the atmosphere of spying and intrigue, now on a European level. Notice that Cromwell and Chapuys both use exactly the same words: 'You have just left him I think.' But More is still politely non-committal. That he is no innocent, but knows what is going on, is shown by his comment 'You are correctly informed. As always.' But he will not be drawn into the corrupt game, although he knows everyone else plays it. Notice that he pays the Boatman what he always pays him; what he considered fair; neither more nor less.

The symbolism of the river, silting up with a deeper channel in the middle, enters again at the end of this scene, as does also the 'common' failing of losing one's 'shape' or identity. By the end of this scene, it is not only the river that begins to look 'black' for More.

Act 1, scene 4

Summary

More, returning home at three o'clock in the morning, finds Roper still there. Roper asks for Margaret's hand in marriage, but More refuses because Roper, as a Lutheran, is a heretic. More refuses to tell either Margaret or Alice what had taken place between himself and Wolsey, but learns he is likely to be Chancellor in place of Wolsey.

Commentary

After the intense political intrigue of the last two scenes, this scene, in More's home, offers some relaxation, even though it shows More in conflict with Roper over the questions of heresy. More's toleration will not extend to accepting a heretic as his son-in-law. But, at the same time, he can still call Roper a 'nice boy'; he recognises the young man's passionate principles, but deals with them, as he does with most other pressure, with calm humour.

The transition to the next scene is one of the most dramatic in the whole play. No sooner has More said 'There will be no new Chancellor while Wolsey lives' than Wolsey's red robe and cardinal's hat are thrown on to the stage, and the Common Man 'roughly piles them into his basket'. The audience had last seen Wolsey in a commanding position, putting pressure on More; now the unceremonious treatment of the 'great red robe' shows how easy it is for great men to fall from favour. So when the Common Man tells the audience about Wolsey's high treason, and then about the new Lord Chancellor, Sir Thomas More, the joke he makes about his 'saintliness' being shown by his 'wilful indifference to realities which were obvious to quite ordinary contemporaries', is double-edged: it tells the audience that More will also fall from favour, and, in spite of his saintliness, 'common' men will find excuses for not defending him.

Act 1, scene 5

Summary

Cromwell reveals to Rich that he is now in the King's service, as the King's 'ear'. In turn, Cromwell, Chapuys and Rich pump the Steward for information about More – but they learn nothing. Cromwell warns Rich that he should 'come in his direction'. We learn that the King is going to visit More at his home to talk about the divorce.

Commentary

Cromwell begins to gain his power over Rich by pretending he doesn't know what Rich's relationship to Norfolk and More is. The word 'friend' has been used earlier in the play between More and Rich: to Cromwell and Rich a 'friend' is someone who can be 'used' to further one's own ends; to More, 'friendship' is a personal and mutual liking and respect between two people. The concept of 'friendship' is raised again between the King and More in the next scene; Cromwell and Rich in the last scene in Act 1; and also between More and Norfolk in Act 2, scene 5. The difference in attitude is at the heart of one important theme of the play – the importance of the individual; no one should exploit or 'use' any other person. It is completely unthinkable for More to 'use' any other person, or allow himself to be 'used' by anyone. Cromwell and Rich, on the other hand, value other people, in money and 'friendship', according to how 'useful' they are.

In this scene, all the characters are assessing how 'useful' the other characters are; first Cromwell and Rich are assessing each other; then Chapuys tries to glean what information he can from Cromwell; then each in turn tries to use the Steward to glean information about More; while the Steward uses them to gain more than he would 'earn in a fortnight'.

Notice Cromwell's disregard and scorn for 'our ancient English constitution', and the satire in 'I merely do things'. Notice, too, how he is annoyed when he finds out how well-informed Chapuys proves to be. Cromwell's comment 'Sir Thomas is a man' implies that he thinks More can be swayed by the King, or forced to change his mind like any other man. But in this case, he doesn't know his 'man'.

The transition to the next scene is again very dramatic. First, the Steward's words to the audience; 'The great thing's not to get out of your depth', and 'Oh, when I can't touch the bottom I'll go deaf, blind and dumb', reflect back to the conversation between the Boatman and More about the river 'silting up' but with 'a channel there getting deeper all the time', and reflect forward to what More is going to do (keep silent) when he finds himself in deep water in the narrow stream where the King and Cromwell have directed nearly everyone else.

So after all the furtive intrigue of the previous scene, and the grim, if humorous, comments of the Steward, the sudden irruption of the 'fanfare of trumpets; plainsong', 'glittering blue light', and screens of 'sunflowers, hollyhocks, roses, magnolias', have a powerful effect on the audience. The trumpets, subconsciously, remind the audience of affairs of state; the plainsong reminds the audience of More's religious and devout character: symbolically, the clash that is going to take place in the next scene has already been set.

Act 1, scene 6

Summary
The King is about to arrive at More's house at Chelsea; More cannot be found; he is discovered, praying, just in time to be made presentable for the King's arrival. After noticing Margaret, the King walks in the garden alone with More, trying to persuade him to agree to the divorce. More will not shift his ground, so the King leaves. Alice upbraids her husband for crossing the King; More replies he has a 'little area' where he must rule himself. Roper and Margaret appear: Roper has been offered a seat in Parliament, and has changed his views on the Church. Rich is announced, warns More that Cromwell is 'collecting information' about him, and asks More to employ him, but More says that Rich couldn't 'answer for himself'. When Rich leaves, Roper and Alice tell More to arrest Rich because he is a dangerous man, but More says there is no law against being a bad man, and defends the law, one thing he is sure about. He tries to reassure Alice that he has not disobeyed any statute or law, nor his King, so he is safe. He makes fun of Roper's 'fine principles'.

Commentary
This scene, the only one in which the King appears in person, is the most theatrically exciting in the play. The excitement is signalled by the fanfare, plainsong, glittering blue light, screens of highly coloured flowers being lowered one after the other, and by Norfolk, Alice and Margaret 'erupting' on to the stage searching for More. The *fanfare*, and the second *fanfare, shorter but nearer*, mean that the King's arrival is imminent. Norfolk's 'He takes things too far', and 'It will end badly for him' sound ominous, although his 'Thomas is unique' makes us realise we are dealing with a very special kind of man.

More's devout nature and humility are shown when is found praying, wearing a simple parish priest's cassock. Bolt deliberately puts More in an undignified situation, and then shows how he keeps his humble dignity when lesser men would have been agitated. That Margaret can *laugh* shows her own identification with her father's calm lack of concern for his undignified appearance.

The entry of Henry, 'in cloth of gold', contrasts completely with More's humility. Henry immediately dictates the tone he wants to establish – regal and authoritative by descending slowly 'to their level', but at the same time playful and friendly by blowing softly on his pilot's whistle. The 'mud' on Henry's shoe is a combination of the water and land images:

More wants to settle things by man's laws (i.e. the road); Henry wants it both ways – legally and with God's (and More's) approval too.

As Henry is made to notice Margaret she is brought to the attention of the audience. When he makes her blow his whistle, the action is an intimation of when, at the end of the play, she will be made, on Henry's orders, to try to make More break his oath. This time, there is 'pleasure all round' when the music breaks out.

When the King and More are alone, the music sets the scene for what is going to be a seduction scene. Henry tries by flattery, appeal, reproof and threat to make More agree to his divorce. Quite purposely, he keeps veering away from the topic, but then comes back to it 'off-hand'. More, however, is unable to agree 'with a clear conscience'. It is More's honesty and sincerity that the King respects, which is why he wants his approval for the divorce. More is 'water in the desert'. But, when More refuses to budge, Henry warns him that 'his conscience is his own'; More can 'lie low' if he wishes, but Henry will 'brook no opposition'.

When Henry leaves 'to catch the tide', More admits to Alice that he had crossed the King because he 'couldn't find the other way'. When Alice tells him he should 'be ruled', More comes to the first definition of his position: 'But there's a little. . .little, area. . .where I must rule myself. It's very little – less to him than a tennis court.' He says this 'pleasantly', without pomp or show, but it is this tiny area of himself that he will not forfeit to anyone, neither his King nor his wife. But that he fully realises the risk is shown by his assurance to Alice that he is not 'the stuff of which martyrs are made'.

When Roper appears and More *winces* 'Oh, no. . .!' we see a human side of him that we rarely see in the play: he has just crossed his King, and his wife, and, for a moment, he feels he cannot stand anything else. But Roper, ironically, says about himself everything that applies to More: 'I'm not easily "told"'; 'I'm full to here! (*Indicates throat*)'; 'I've got an inconvenient conscience'; and 'My spirit is perturbed'. More would never *say* these things about himself, but he feels them, and Roper says them for him; so when Margaret gestures to her father, he quickly recovers his good humour. However, Roper, not knowing what had happened between More and the King, and being insensitive to what More is feeling, accuses him of sophistication, of being corrupted by the court, and of studying his own convenience. All this, however, More takes in good turn.

When Rich appears, he warns More that Cromwell is collecting information about him, and asks More to employ him because he's 'adrift', the audience is meant to compare these two young men who here meet for the first time. More will not trust Rich because he is not 'steadfast' and cannot 'answer for himself'; to Roper, More says later: 'Will, I'd trust *you* with my life. But not your principles.' Roper, as a person, is 'steadfast', even if his 'views' and 'principles' change.

When More refuses to arrest Rich, More's own position in relation to the law, and to God is explained. More, using the water symbolism, says he can't navigate in 'the currents and eddies of right and wrong' – that's God's affair, and later that, although God is his god: '(*Rather bitter*.) But I find him rather too (*very bitter*) subtle. . .I don't know where he is nor what he wants.' Notice the stage directions, and Bolt's use of capitals and lower case letters in his references to God. More's religious position is nearer to being agnostic than that of a devout Catholic. His objection to the King's divorce is not through a God-given sense of 'right or wrong'. Neither is it a matter of 'principle', as he shows by making fun of Roper's 'seagoing principles'. What More says he does understand better than any man alive (with a small show of professional pride) is the 'thickets' of Man's law, which he implies, save us from 'the winds' of anarchy, chaos and injustice.

It is only when More says that he is going to hide himself and his daughter in these thickets, that Roper realises More is being 'hunted'; and here, although More is 'harsh' towards Roper (again showing a chink of human weakness), Roper shows his trustworthiness as a man by taking no offence, but immediately showing his concern. More, realising his harshness to Roper, comes back (*a little sheepish*) to apologise, but he still can't resist sending him up on his very best quality 'principles', and he can't resist asking if Roper's 'principles' will permit him to drink Burgundy, and then, *laughing*, and *inviting Roper to laugh with him*, commenting how 'principles', although 'anchored', can be shifted 'if the weather turns nasty'.

By the end of this scene, which is the last time we see More in the first Act, we know that he will be 'hunted' and his defence will be the 'thickets of the law'.

The transition further implicates the audience, as 'common' men and women, in the indifference shown by 'loyal subjects' to the fate of brave men who go against the tide. The name of the pub, The Loyal Subject, is ironic; we feel guilty about being loyal in a case like this. The Common Man's excuse is that More is too deep for him to follow: '(*Deadpan*.) The likes of me can hardly be expected to follow the processes of a man like that. . .', then the change to the plural really implicates the audience: '(*Sly*.) Can we?' We are all too busy with our own affairs to bother for long. Having settled that, we are ready for the hunting of More.

Act 1, scene 7

Summary
Cromwell, who has become secretary to the Council, continues the corruption of Rich by making him Collector of Revenues for York Diocese. Having made him slightly drunk, Cromwell asks him about the silver goblet More gave Rich. Rich realises this evidence is going to be used against More. Rich protests that More is an 'innocent' and 'doesn't know how to be frightened'. Cromwell replies by holding Rich's hand in the candle flame.

Commentary
This scene establishes how ruthless, irreligious, unprincipled – in a word, Machiavellian – More's hunters are. The Common Man, in the guise of the Publican, tries not to implicate himself by pretending to be innocent of what is going on. So do most of the 'common' people of the audience who earlier identified themselves with the Common Man's 'Can we?'

Cromwell shows his disrespect for his King by his take-off of Henry's mannerisms and sayings: 'No ceremony, no courtship. Be seated.' He also says this to show his own power, and to test Rich. 'Friendship' is mentioned again, and Cromwell's 'If you like' shows that 'friendship' has no real meaning for him – it's just a matter of convenience. Cromwell's repetition of 'seriously' (*Not sinister, but rather as a kindly teacher with a promising pupil*) makes him all that more sinister, dangerous and devilish. (The Devil rarely appears in sinister guises.) His amorality comes out in this dialogue with Rich, although he says he admires Rich for being honest and open about his 'price' by asking, 'It would depend what I was offered.' The real 'price' for this is hinted at in the stage directions – *bitterly, suspicious, gripping on to himself, conscious cynicism*, etc.: he is quite consciously selling his 'soul' or 'self'. (More himself later equates the 'soul' to the 'self'.) But Rich has just the faintest doubts, expressed in his: 'There are *some* things one wouldn't do for anything. Surely.' (When people say 'Surely', they often mean they are not really sure.) And when Cromwell asks if he is sure he is not religious, his answer 'Almost sure' also expresses his doubt. Unlike Cromwell, Rich is not amoral; he knows he is doing wrong.

This, like the previous scene between More and the King, is a seduction scene; but Rich is an easy victim. He finally gives up having any twinges of conscience when he agrees (*much struck*) that the loss of his innocence had not meant much to him: after this he *takes wine* and begins to relax. The stage directions in this scene are very important, because they reveal a secondary, unspoken dialogue going on, with Cromwell completely in control of how the scene will develop – until the very last seconds.

The 'lecture' which Cromwell gives on 'administrative convenience' is directed at the modern audience as well as at Rich. By laughing, they show their potential for corruption, as Rich demonstrates by being *pleased*, *waving his cup*, and providing the right answer at the end of the lecture.

Once Cromwell has hooked Rich, the dialogue becomes brisk and businesslike on the subject of the silver goblet. This, Rich soon realises, is going to be evidence used against More, and he is *a little rueful* and *unhappy*. Rich's sense of guilt at the realisation that his 'little titbits of information' are going to be used against More, is shown by his not being able to look up, and by the way he tries to plead that More is an 'innocent' who 'doesn't know how to be frightened'. But his face is *nasty* when he says this. He knows, even at this stage, that no matter how much he admires More, he is going to allow himself to be 'used' against him, if this means his own advancement.

The psychological tensions at the end of this scene are involved and interesting. Both men are screwing themselves up to destroy a man whom they know to be innocent. All the worst characteristics come out in both of them, and the sadistic act of holding Rich's hand in the candle flame, amazes even Cromwell himself, as the stage direction shows. But this act of cruelty at the end of the first Act, gives the audience a foretaste of what is to come.

Act 2, Prologue

Summary
The Common Man explains that the time has moved on from 1530 to May, 1532, and in the intervening years the Church of England had been established by an Act of Parliament.

Commentary
The new Act begins, as did the first Act, with the Common Man in a single spotlight. The tone now is purposely ironic and comic. After their relaxation during the interval, Bolt wants the members of the audience to be united once again, and involved in the play by the humour on stage. The Common Man's spectacles make him a ludicrous figure when wearing his tights, and his *explanatory* 'Two years', brings a laugh because it is so obvious. The transfer from the Common Man's own comment to the reading from the 'book' enables Bolt to be even more ironic about the 'unhappy few', and 'an age less fastidious than our own': what he means

is that 'imprisonment without trial', and 'examination under torture' are still common practice. But the comment here, though raising a wry smile, prepares us for More's fate.

Act 2, scene 1

Summary

More tells Roper, who is dressed in black and wearing a cross to show his allegiance to the Catholic Church – in contrast to his allegiance to Luther at the beginning of the first Act, that he will forfeit his chain of office as Chancellor if the Bishops in Convocation (in session that morning) agree to the Act of Supremacy which made the King 'Protector and Only Supreme Head of the Church and Clergy of England'. More tries to hide his own opinion on this behind the clause 'so far as the law of God allows'. Chapuys appears with Margaret, and when Roper and Margaret have left, flatters More as the 'English Socrates'. He says More's resignation will be seen as a 'signal' of dissent to Catholics in the North of England, and abroad. Roper, Norfolk, Margaret and Alice enter, and Norfolk announces that Convocation had 'knuckled under'. Chapuys stays long enough to see More put his hand to his chain, which is removed by Margaret after Alice had vehemently refused to have a hand in her husband's resignation. In reply to Norfolk's request to make him understand More's position, More explained that the tenuous theory that the Pope was the only link with Christ was important to him because *he* believed it. To show the danger of the times, and that he was afraid, More tricks Norfolk into denying his oath of obedience to the King; but Norfolk assures them that the King will respect More's 'honour and welfare'. More warns Norfolk of Chapuys' visit to the North. When Norfolk leaves, Alice upbraids More, who is annoyed when Roper says he has made a 'noble gesture', and done a 'moral' (not a practical) act. When Margaret tries to placate her father, Alice turns on Margaret, Roper and More, because she realises he will not be left alone. More argues that so long as he keeps his silence and makes no statement on the King's supremacy to anyone, he will be safe. More asks the Steward to stay on for a smaller wage: the Steward refuses.

Commentary

In this first scene of the new Act, the events of the last two years have to be explained quickly. The Act opens with More on the very last morning of his material prosperity. (The first Act had seen his rise; this Act will see his fall.) He once again makes fun of Roper's earnestness in wearing black clothes and a cross to show he is a Catholic; but Roper shows his uneasiness by pacing up and down. The point that Roper makes about 'decent men declaring their allegiance' is valid for any time and place, and thousands of men and women through the ages have died and suffered because they have done so. Roper in turn accuses More of hiding behind the 'legal quibble' of the ambiguity of the clause 'so far as the law of God allows'. More will not tell Roper his own opinion of this, and warns Roper not to do so either for fear of his being accused of treason. This clearly warns the audience that the 'times' have become more dangerous.

Chapuys' reference to Erasmus, and his later word 'signal', make the audience realise that More's stand had European significance by showing his dissent to Catholics in other countries; it is not just a personal matter. It is significant that when Chapuys gives his blessing to Margaret and Roper he now includes the words 'filii mei' (my children) of the Catholic rather than the Protestant Church. Chapuys' flattery has no effect on More, but when he is left alone with More, he makes him *agitated* because he very cleverly comes to the very nub of More's dilemma: 'There comes a point. . . [when] one is not merely "compromised", one is in truth corrupted.' When More asks Chapuys what he wanted, he expected Chapuys to ask for some sign of betrayal of his King and country (which More would never have contemplated), so when he says no more than that More would resign the chancellorship (which we already know he was going to do), More regains his composure and can be *suave* in his replies. But notice he *looks down* throughout the next exchanges, so as not to give away his feelings, even at the word 'signal'. It is only when Chapuys says that More's stand will be seen as a signal for 'resistance' (a very modern word) by his fellow countrymen (i.e. an insurrection) that More *looks up sharply*. This is a new danger for More. As he is universally known as a good and temperate man, his refusal to state his opinion on the King's supremacy will be seen as a 'signal' for Catholics in the North of England to raise a rebellion – as they did two years later. His personal opinion, which concerns himself alone, has wider ramifications.

It is dramatically effective that just at this moment Roper bursts in, announcing the entry of Norfolk, and blurting out 'It's all over'. But Norfolk wants to be the one to give More the news that 'Convocation's knuckled under'. Notice that Norfolk enters *above*, so when Chapuys exits *up stairs*, the two have to cross, which is why Norfolk comments to More that this is 'funny company' at such time (and in the next scene he reports this visit to Cromwell). When Norfolk comments 'And. . . we've severed the connection with Rome', More repeats this twice (*bitter*), because for him, as we see later, it severed his belief in the 'only link with Christ'.

This is the crucial moment of decision for More, but he can still praise Bishop Fisher, and make a pun on the word 'funny'. The taking off of his chain of office is the symbol of his having 'come to the point' beyond which he was not prepared to go. But he merely fumbles with the chain and wants help, 'morally', to take it off. Norfolk refuses, More will not accept Roper's help, Alice vehemently refuses, but Margaret accepts, showing the greatest trust and simplicity with the words 'If you want.'

Norfolk's request to make him understand because it looked like cowardice, makes More mention the 'hawks' again, and although More says he is not one of them (i.e. lacking in caution), in another way he is, because he is also courageous, which is why Norfolk's accusation of 'cowardice' makes him *excited and angry*. It also makes him declare his reason, and the stage direction, *Stops interested*, makes it seem as if he is thinking this out for himself for the first time: 'Why, it's a theory yes; you can't see it; can't touch it; it's a theory. (*To* Norfolk, *very rapid but calm*.) But what matters to me is not whether it's true or not but that I believe it to be true, or rather not that I *believe* it, but that *I* believe it. . .I trust I make myself obscure?' The important word is the italicised *I*.

Bolt has been criticised for making More take such an individualistic stand. Freedom of conscience, that a man should be free to believe whatever he likes, whether that belief takes religious, political or any other form, is at the heart of the play. (That More condemns Roper during his Lutheran stage is part of More's narrow-minded historical trappings.) But, in fact Bolt was not so far out: a few decades later Christopher Marlowe's Jew of Malta could say, 'I am myself alone'; Shakespeare's Hamlet could say, 'The time is out of joint; O, cursed spite/That ever I was born to put it right' – with, once again, the emphasis on the *I*. Consciousness of the boundaries of the individual 'self' was a part of Renaissance thinking. But the point that Bolt is making here is that it doesn't matter whether the 'theory' More believed in was religious, political or scientific, he would forfeit everything for the right to believe it. Even here, More can be witty, by changing 'I trust I make myself clear' to 'I trust I make myself obscure', which sounds much more modern than sixteenth-century; and then the quick-fire pun on 'obscurity' (meaning 'out of the public eye') would not be out of place in a Tom Stoppard play.

Norfolk thinks More is sick if he seeks obscurity (in the above sense) when he is such a well-loved and respected man; he is not in danger of being persecuted, as he would be in Spain. (When this play was being written in the late 1950s the Committee on Un-American Activities was sitting in the USA, and many prominent people were sent to prison for refusing to 'testify' about their activities or those of their friends.) But More immediately demonstrates to Norfolk, by trapping him into denying his oath of obedience, just how dangerous the times are, and Norfolk's reassurance that More should have no fear is answered by More *flatly*; he doesn't believe it, because he is more shrewdly aware of the dangers. But when More, showing his patriotism, warns Norfolk of Chapuys' tour of the North, his tone changes to *briskly professional*, and he shows a *flash of jealousy* when he finds that Cromwell had proved equally professional. He then changes to *anger* when Norfolk doubts his patriotism. In fact, this scene, by its swift changes in mood and tone, is a great test for an actor.

When Norfolk has left, Alice, the realist, turns on her husband; seeing where More's studies have led him, she shows her scorn for learning. Roper can see More's stand only as a 'noble gesture', which alarms More, especially when Roper tries to explain it is 'moral' not 'practical'. Bolt is saying here that our practical, day-to-day lives should be governed by morality – and not, as for most of us, as an afterthought shown by occasional 'gestures'. Even Margaret pleads that this practical morality is too much for most people; so More gets no real understanding or sympathy from any of his family, and Alice turns his accusation of cruelty against himself, and then turns on both Margaret and Roper for supporting More in his foolishness (as she sees it), which she knows, intuitively, will cost him his life ('dance him to the block'). To her, for all his intelligence, her husband is no more than a 'poor, silly man', and the audience is made to realise that Alice, with her anger, is wiser than More, for all his legal cleverness and circumspection. William Blake's aphorism; 'The tigers of wrath are wiser than the horses of instruction' gave Bolt the title of his next play, *The Tiger and the Horse*.

The arrival of the Steward signals the end of the scene, and the beginning of More's straitened circumstances, which, as Alice comments, 'comes on us quickly'. More tries to treat his relationship with the Steward on a personal level, but the Steward takes this as a trick to try to get him to take a lower wage. The word 'them' (i.e. the employing or ruling class) shows that the Steward, just in time, dismisses any consideration of a personal relationship with More, but sees it in terms of labour and wages. When the Common Man takes off his Steward's coat, picks up his hat and draws the curtain to the alcove, these actions signify the end of his stewardship – and the end of More's prosperity.

Act 2, scene 2

Summary

Norfolk advises Cromwell to let More stay silent, but Cromwell says More's silence is 'bellowing up and down Europe'. Cromwell ascertains that More had reported to Norfolk on Chapuys' visit to the North of England, so he must be against Spain and for England, and must be made to say so. Cromwell thinks pressure can be brought on More because he accepted bribes (which is vehemently denied by Norfolk), and produces Rich and the woman who had given the silver goblet to More. Norfolk realises it was the goblet he had seen More give to Rich just because it was meant as a bribe and More wanted none of it. So this attempt to put pressure on More fails. Norfolk says he wants no part in making More break his silence, but Cromwell puts pressure on Norfolk by saying that the King particularly wants Norfolk, as a known friend of More, to participate. Norfolk is furious at being threatened by Cromwell, and leaves. Cromwell rebukes Rich for not remembering the details about the silver goblet and says they must trap More by law, and if there isn't a suitable law, then they must make one. When Cromwell leaves, Rich takes on the Common Man as his Steward.

Commentary

Before this scene started, Norfolk had obviously reported to Cromwell what More had told him about Chapuys' visit to the North of England; he had, possibly, wanted to demonstrate to Cromwell that More, although a 'crank', was no traitor. But Cromwell uses this to put the propostion that 'if he opposes Spain, he supports us, with no possibility of a third alternative'. (In the next scene, Chapuys is made to echo this: 'If he's opposed to Cromwell, he's for us. There's no third alternative.') Cromwell wants pressure brought on More to say so, because his 'silence is bellowing up and down Europe'. Norfolk, being a true friend to More, doesn't want to be implicated in bringing pressure on More to break his silence, so Cromwell now has to start using pressure on Norfolk by saying that the King does not agree with letting More stay silent, and then by producing Rich and the woman who had given the silver goblet to More as a bribe. (Notice that Norfolk gives Rich a *savage snub* when he says they were 'old friends'.) Cromwell had obviously rehearsed this case carefully, because he consults the paper on which the details were written. Norfolk's trust in More is shown by his incredulous disbelief in the thought of his ever having taken bribes. But Cromwell tries to corroborate his evidence by calling on Rich (who had been given the goblet by More), who says he can produce a witness in More's former Steward. (The fickleness of 'the common man' is demonstrated by his willingness to turn so quickly against his former master.) But Norfolk had also been a witness when the goblet was given (which Rich had forgotten), so Norfolk is *triumphant* when he realises his faith in More is justified.

Norfolk is *between bullying and plea* because although he knows that 'this horse won't run', he inevitably realises that his friendship for More is going to be 'used' by Cromwell. Although Norfolk says he 'wants no part in this' (i.e. putting pressure on More), he knows he is caught. Now Cromwell puts direct pressure on Norfolk, saying that he has no choice because the King particularly wished Norfolk to show his participation, as a loyal friend of More's, in making More state his allegiance. It must also be seen publicly that what is being done is according to the strict processes of the law and is not 'persecution'. (What Bolt has been showing in these two scenes is the cruel pressure that a good man who stands by his beliefs can put on his family, and his friends.) When Norfolk furiously asks Cromwell if he is being threatened, Cromwell, ironically, uses exactly the same words as Norfolk had used to More in the previous scene: 'This isn't Spain.'

When this attempt to ensnare More fails, Cromwell looks for another approach. In the previous scene, More had explained that he was using his silence as a legal 'life-line' – 'in silence is my safety under the law' and 'I know what's legal not what's right. And I'll stick to what's legal.' Cromwell decides to attempt to attack More on his strong point, law; but when he says to Rich: 'You're absolutely right, it must be done by law', the stage direction (*Straight-faced*) tells us that he is telling a lie: this is not Rich's idea, but his own, but he is trying to make Rich think that it did come from him so he can more deeply implicate Rich in this 'legal' manoeuvre. (It is, later, Rich, not Cromwell, who perjures himself.) The lack of respect in which Rich and Cromwell hold the law is shown by Rich's *uncertain* statement: 'I'm only anxious to do what is correct', and by Cromwell's comment that if they can't find the right law, they will make one. To him, the law is an instrument to be manipulated at will.

When Rich takes on Matthew as his Steward at the end of the scene, it shows, symbolically, that as More goes down socially, Rich goes up. But the Common Man shows he knows exactly how to handle Rich. He flatters him with the suggestion that he has now 'risen to his proper level'; but when Rich has gone, the Common Man's comment 'Oh, I can manage this one! He's just my size!' makes us realise he and Rich are in some ways alike: neither has any 'little piece of ground' which he can call his 'self'. They will both shift their ground just as it suits them. But Rich is ambitious, whereas the Common Man is not.

Act 2, scene 3

Summary

Alice enters with Chapuys and an Attendant. Before Alice goes she asks Chapuys, who has a Royal Commission to perform, to leave before her husband comes. Chapuys tells the attendant, 'If he's opposed to Cromwell, he's for us.' When More enters, asking if the visit is personal or official, Chapuys says he has a personal letter from King Charles. More refuses to take it. When Chapuys says More's views are 'well-known', More protests they are 'much guessed at', but his loyalty to his country is less well-known.

Margaret enters with a large bundle of bracken, and when Alice enters, More uses them as witnesses to see that the letter was unopened and returned to Chapuys, who leaves with the Attendant, saying More is 'utterly unreliable'. Alice scoffs at More's suggestion that a bracken fire is 'luxury'. Neither Alice nor Margaret can persuade More to take the four thousand pounds raised by the Bishops because More thinks it would appear dangerous to have been in the pay of the Church. Roper enters and says More is to answer certain charges before Cromwell at Hampton Court. Alice is distressed and says Cromwell is a 'nimble lawyer', but More protests he is just a pragmatist.

Commentary

Alice's entry *wearing a big coarse apron* reinforces the Common Man's words, 'Sir Thomas More's again gone down a bit', and Bolt also emphasises this by asking for a lighting change to make the set look 'drab and chilly'. That Chapuys and the Attendant are *cloaked* brings an air of intrigue, but when Chapuys wraps his cloak about him, it serves to emphasise the cold even further. Although the interlude between Chapuys and the Attendant serves us a moment of light relief, it also raises the important point 'goodness presents its own difficulties'. When Chapuys mirrors Cromwell's proposition to Norfolk about More ('If he's opposed to Cromwell, he's for us. There's no third alternative.'), More is seen to be isolated from both sides. For him it isn't a matter of being 'for' or 'against'.

When More appears, he moves *rather more deliberately than before*. This contrasts with Bolt's original comment on More in the list of People in the Play: 'His movements are open and swift'. His straitened circumstances, and the worry he is causing his family and friends, are taking their toll on him physically. Chapuys' comment on More's 'stand', and his views being 'well-known', again show how More's silence is open to misinterpretation. But he shows that his loyalty to the crown is not in doubt by his refusal to touch the letter from King Charles of Spain. (Agents of foreign powers are always anxious to recruit influential people who are in trouble or disillusioned with their own country; but More could never conceive of being disloyal to his country.)

Margaret's entry with *a huge bundle of bracken* is a masterly stroke of theatre, but the bundle must be really huge; the audience must gasp and laugh at its size. There is some historical evidence for this bracken (see page 52), but why did Bolt choose to use this incident? It symbolises the family's attitude to poverty. To More, Margaret and Roper (who later enters with a sickle), there is 'sport' in collecting such huge bundles. Margaret's, 'Look, Father! Will's getting more!' is said with childish delight; and More's response, 'Oh, well done...Is it dry? Oh it is!' is said without whimsy and with equal delight. With their innocence they have become 'as little children' and are finding delight in poverty. The audience can imagine the quick , hot fire of the bracken, with its flames and sparks, and More's and Margaret's pleasure while it lasts, honestly finding it a 'luxury'. But to the practical Alice, this is just foolishness; she *kicks the bracken* and *sits wearily* on the bundle: and to Chapuys, who can manage only a *cold smile*, More's delight in such simple pleasures shows that he is 'utterly unreliable'.

But the *huge bundle of bracken* does more than this. Apart from showing how much time and effort the poor have to spend to obtain the necessities of life – *they're cold and their interest in fuel is serious* – the dry bracken is a symbol of the vanity of life itself. What More (and Bolt) are saying is that it is better to go up in one big, clean, fierce flame, than smoulder away smokily. Margaret and Roper can understand this; but, it is madness to Alice and Chapuys.

Having accepted this, Alice has no reason to hope that her husband will accept the four thousand pounds collected by the clergy, even though, here, Margaret sides with her mother and thinks her father should accept. There is historical evidence that such a large sum (worth about one hundred times the amount in modern currency) had been collected, and it is further evidence of More's esteem and popularity, which made him all the more dangerous to Cromwell – and to the King.

More is quite truthful when he says he could have been merry as a beggar, but it is because of his family that he wants to keep out of danger. But he has no sooner said that he doesn't think there is any danger and that he doesn't want there to be, when Roper comes in saying that More is to answer certain charges before Cromwell. Alice and Margaret are right to be *appalled*, and More is *not very convincing* when he says he expected this.

The lighting is used to isolate More even further from his family, leaving them in the dark – both on the stage and metaphorically. Margaret shows her bravery and devotion to her father by wanting to go with him; but More, even in this moment of tension and danger, can be witty - both in his threat to bring Cromwell home to dinner, and for the pun on the word 'wit'. He can also show another little flash of professional pride in his own expertise in the law as compared with Cromwell. But that he calls Cromwell a 'pragmatist' is cruel irony, because, later, Cromwell is to use the law in a Machiavellian way for his own purposes.

Act 2, scene 4

Summary

More attends the summons to Hampton Court to answer Cromwell's 'charges'. Cromwell reveals that Rich is there to record the proceedings. Cromwell first tries to bring More round by saying he is going against the universities, the bishops, Parliament, and the King. More replies *stonily*. Cromwell then raises the case of the 'Holy Maid of Kent', accusing More of not warning the King of her treason. More replies that both his conversation with the woman, and a letter he wrote to her, were not political, and they were both witnessed. Cromwell, realising that More has covered himself, turns to his third 'charge'. He accuses More of having written or instigated the King's book *A Defence of the Seven Sacraments*, published in May, 1521, which sets out and defends the Pope's authority (which, of course, the King now denies). More retorts that this charge is 'trivial' because, under oath, the King would never perjure himself by denying his part in the book. Cromwell then asks More if he has anything further to say on the King's marriage to Queen Anne. More replies that he had understood he was not to be asked again, and says these are 'terrors for children'. Cromwell, in the King's name, charges More with 'great ingratitude' and with being a 'villainous servant' and a 'traitorous subject'. More realises he had been 'brought here at last'. Cromwell allows him to go home, 'for the present'.

Cromwell now agrees with Rich that More cannot be frightened. Cromwell and Rich had made themselves the keepers of the King's conscience, which demanded that More has either to bless his marriage, or be destroyed.

Commentary

This is the first scene in the play which does not have some prologue or transition provided by the Common Man. The effect is to plunge More straight into the scene with Cromwell without the cushion of humour usually provided. This speeds up More's destruction, giving neither More, nor the audience, breathing space. Cromwell's polite comments are completely hypocritical. He thinks that he has More in his power so he reveals Rich who records the conversation.

More's comment to Rich that they were 'old friends' takes us back to the very first scene in the play, where Rich had asked if he could be More's 'friend'. He had also said he wanted a gown like More's; but More's comment in this scene about Rich's 'nice gown' should be made without any bitterness or sarcasm.

Cromwell, however, is being sarcastic when he comments that it is asking too much to ask More to believe him: he knows, and More knows, that nothing he says need be believed. Cromwell doesn't want it recorded that he had said he was one of More's sincerest admirers because it might later be used in evidence against him; but Rich shows his political ineptitude by recording this. These are just polite formalities. More tries to bring Cromwell abruptly to the point by asking to hear the 'charges', and he is quick, with a flash of ironic humour (which Cromwell appreciates), to ask Rich to record that there are no charges. He is also quick to take up the word 'charge' again when Cromwell lets it slip out 'for want of a better word'.

As soon as the 'charges' are read out, More shows that, legally, he is more than a match for Cromwell. His dealings with the 'holy Maid of Kent' had been carefully witnessed. On the matter of the King's book, he knows better than Cromwell that the King will not perjure himself. Cromwell resorts to charging More, in the King's name, with being a traitor. More's 'So I am brought here at last', shows that, in spite of his faith in the law, this is what he had been expecting all along.

Cromwell's *official* dismissal is ominous: 'You may go home now. For the present.' His metaphor about More, 'There's a man who raises the gale and won't come out of harbour' shows the storms that More's silence has caused; but yet More remains calm. This is also the cue for the rear of the stage to become *water patterned* which means that, within the water metaphor that runs through the play, the next little scene between Rich and Cromwell, which is the acme of the legal chicanery – 'We'll do whatever's necessary' – is played against a background which symbolises More's integrity. Cromwell here shows himself a master of Machiavellian argument: his logic is faultless. But Rich is *shaky* and *subdued*; he is still learning the political game.

Act 2, scene 5

Summary
More, unable to hire a boat, is purposely overtaken by Norfolk, who tells More he's behaving like a fool. Norfolk is being used in a policy against More, so More says Norfolk must stop being his friend because of his obedience to the King, and because of his son. Norfolk says this is impossible; More must give in, like everyone else. More says this is impossible. Norfolk says More will break his heart. More says they must part as friends and meet as strangers. When Norfolk says this is daft, More tries to insult Norfolk about his class, about water spaniels, about his denial of his self, and about his pedigree. Norfolk retaliates by lashing out, and leaves, but not before Margaret has seen this. Roper enters and says there is a new Act of Parliament about administering an oath on the King's marriage. More says they must study the words of the oath. He explains to Margaret and Roper that one must escape if possible, but if God brought one to the extremity of no escape, then He must delight in the splendour that Man can show.

Commentary

As in the last change of scene, the Common Man is not used to make the transition, but this time he is conspicuous by his absence, because, previously, when More had called for a boat, he had appeared as the Boatman. Now More is so isolated, and such a dangerous person to know, that not even a boatman will come to take him home.

This scene is the climax of the theme of friendship that has run through the play. More and Norfolk are the only true friends in the play. They are not friends for any purpose, expediency, reason or use – as are the other 'friendships'. Although there are many reasons why it seems strange that they are such good friends (differences of class, outlook, intellect, etc.), as Norfolk says: I'm fond of you, and there it is! You're fond of me, and there it is!' One thing Bolt is saying in the play is that in friendship there are no ulterior motives.

But another thing that Bolt is saying in this scene is that a good man can cause pain not only to his family, but to his friends. Norfolk's statement: 'You'll break my heart' is one of the most emotionally charged moments in the play. The stage direction for these few words is *Quiet and quick*. A man of Norfolk's class, more used to showing a stiff upper lip, should not show his emotions – particularly to another man. But here it is forced out of Norfolk, quietly and quickly, and More is *moved*, because he knows from what depths this simple statement had forced itself up, against all Norfolk's upbringing and training. But as More had put aside the appeal of his family, so, although he is moved, he puts aside the appeal of his friend. That small piece of his 'self' cannot give in.

The scene begins by making it clear that Norfolk, for the sake of friendship, had taken some risk to be seen with More. He *looks back*, *off*, when he says he followed More; and when asked if he was followed, replies 'Probably'. Even so, his friendship for More is such that he must attempt to save him – as he sees it. (The scene ends with More trying to save Norfolk – as *he* sees it.) Norfolk's appeal to More as a 'gentleman' does not impress More because he has no pretensions about being a 'gentleman'. But More fully understands the pressure that is being put on Norfolk as More's friend. (We have already had this demonstrated in the scene between Norfolk, Cromwell and Rich.) More immediately thinks of Norfolk's family and property ('You have a son'), because if Norfolk were accused of high treason (as he later was), not only his own life, but his title and property would be forfeited, and More knows this is important to such a 'gentleman' as Norfolk. His reaction is to tell Norfolk that he must stop knowing him as a friend, but to Norfolk this is impossible: 'You might as well advise a man to change the colour of his hair!' Norfolk replies, *with deep appeal*, that More must 'give in'. But More replies, *gently*, that this is impossible: '(*smile*) You might as well advise a man to change the colour of his eyes.'

With this moving, but witty exchange, we come to the crux of More's position, which he is *urgent to explain* to his friend (whom he addresses by his family name, Howard, many times in this scene, although he does so very rarely elsewhere in the play). His first attempt: 'Affection goes as deep in me as you I think, but only God is love right through, Howard; and *that's* my *self*' is not easy to understand, and the italics show that he is having difficulty in explaining himself. More has shown how deep his affection for Norfolk does go; but even deeper, so that it goes right through the core (or 'heart'), is a man's relationship with 'God'. This is a metaphor, or an equivalent, for the relationship with his own 'self'. Not only God, but each individual, should judge every moment of his life: in fact, the 'self' who judges is 'God'.

To Norfolk, this looks 'disproportionate' and 'arrogant'. (By '*We*', in italics, he means the 'nobility'.) But after his *quiet and quick* confession, More does not, as yet, attempt to explain himself again. He tries to take what he thinks is the practical step of shaking hands 'as friends, and meet as strangers', but to Norfolk this is just 'daft'. So More realises that the only way to save Norfolk is to break their friendship by insulting him. He *takes a last affectionate look at him* then *walks away*. He tries to distance himself from Norfolk, both physically and metaphorically. (But notice that later in the scene he *goes up to him and feels him up and down like an animal*.) He then tries to insult Norfolk by saying his class is more interested in a dog's pedigree than in religion – but even here he can't stop being witty. But Norfolk protests this is just an 'artificial quarrel'. More's comment that their 'friendship was but sloth' (notice he uses the past tense 'was') is cruel; but Norfolk can take even this. More is then wittily vindictive with the sarcastically alliterative invented names for the dogs 'marsh mastiffs' and 'bog beagles'. But considering the nature of a water spaniel takes him back to the essential nature of a man, and to Norfolk, and his second attempt to explain himself: 'Well, as a spaniel is to water, so is a man to his own self. I will not give in because I oppose it – *I* do – not my pride, not my spleen, nor any other of my appetites but *I* do – I!' Here Margaret's voice is heard off-stage, and More's *attention is irrestistibly caught by this*; but he must still attempt to save Norfolk (whom he no longer calls by Family name), and his final appeal to Norfolk gives the clearest indication of what More means by a person's 'self': 'Is there no single sinew in the midst of this that serves no appetite of Norfolk's but is, just, Norfolk? There is! Give *that* some exercise, my Lord!' He wants Norfolk to get 'right through' to his essential 'self', because until he does find his true 'self' which can judge his own life, 'you'll go before your Maker in a very ill condition!'

At this highly charged moment Margaret enters, but *she stops, amazed at them*. But More has still to break his friendship with Norfolk, so he delivers his final insult, which, wittily, is an insult to Norfolk's own pedigree. More knows this is the greatest insult to a member of the nobility. At last Norfolk *lashes out at him*, and More *ducks and winces*. But, ironically, this final cruel insult comes from the depths of More's affection for Norfolk: he has tried to save his 'soul', and he must also try to save his life and property. The stage directions after Norfolk has left, even when Margaret and Roper are attempting, excitedly, to gain his attention, show how much this had cost More: *Looks after him wistfully*; *still looking off, unanswering*; *the same*; *half-turning, half attending*; *indifferent*; *turning back again*. It is only when Margaret *puts hand on his arm* and tells him about an 'oath' that he gives his *instantaneous attention*. He is then *very still* when he asks about the oath, and still, with his legal training and hope of escape, he wants to know the 'wording', because, to More, the words of an oath are important because it is the 'self' which takes the oath.

Even when he realises they have no boat, *he looks off again* after Norfolk. But Norfolk has gone and his isolation is complete. Margaret, realising her father is thinking of Norfolk, asks *gently* what happened, but More dismisses it lightly with his usual wit. All the same, he now, in spite of wanting to see the 'wording', realises that there is 'no escaping', and he explains his position to Margaret and Roper. (Alice, notice, is not present.)

In this fine speech, which is not one based on More's own words, but is, as Bolt said in his interviews with Ronald Hayman 'All My Own Work', Bolt uses the concept of what E. M. W. Tillyard in his book *The Elizabethan World Picture* called 'The Great Chain of Being', that is, man's place in the universe as conceived by the sixteenth-century mind. At the head was God, then the angels, then man, then animals, plants, and so on, all in order. Man was the crucial link between heaven and earth, between the angels and the animals. The best part of man, his 'self' or 'soul' (as More later calls it), aspires towards the angels; the grosser part of man, which serves his appetites, is nearer the animals. This is why More feels Norfolk *up and down like an animal* when he is searching for that 'single sinew in the midst of this that serves no appetite of Norfolk's but is, just, Norfolk'. He is searching for Norfolk's 'self' or 'soul'.

In this speech More suggests that Man's distinctive way to serve God is to use his reason and intellect to try to sort out the complexities of his life on earth, but, at the same time, keep his 'self' intact: otherwise he is nothing. Man should naturally use his intellect to preserve himself, but if God brings a man into a position from which there is no escaping, then it no doubt delights God to see a man leaving all the demands of worldly appetites behind him, and showing the splendour of his angel-like qualities – if he has the courage to do this.

Transition

Summary

A rack descends and remains suspended. A cage is lowered to the floor. The Common Man enters as a Jailer. Behind the table he sets up three chairs, which are taken by Cromwell, Norfolk and Archbishop Cranmer, the three members of the Commission. Rich stands behind them. More enters and lies down in the cage. The Common Man reveals the subsequent fate of the members of the Commission.

Commentary

After two scene changes without the Common Man, he now comes into his own again, as a Jailer. Is Bolt commenting that, in the last analysis, it is the common men, in any country, in any age, who allow good men to suffer, because of their complicity in the punishment? As the Common

Man says: 'I'd let him out if I could but I can't. Not without taking up residence in there myself. And he's in there already, so what'd be the point?' His off-hand, dismissive, colloquial style shows that he knows he is not fulfilling his 'obligations' (a word which is later used about More, who did fulfil all his obligations) as a man, but is trying to convince himself that there is nothing he can do about it.

The suspended rack, although never used, is a real reminder that physical torture has been, and still is, used against prisoners, particularly in cases of 'conscience'. The cage is the symbol of imprisonment itself. That the Common Man *turns and watches the completion of the transformation* of the stage into a prison, makes it seem that he wants to have no part in it. And his *aggrieved* tone, and his *shrug*, are further attempts to shake off responsibility. His quotation of the old adage, and comment 'and that's about it', is a further attempt to dismiss the subject of his responsibility.

But the swift descent of the envelope (sent from God? Or from the Fates?) is an immediate ironical comment on the truth not only of the 'adage', but also of the rest of his comments. And the message itself is highly ironical: three members of the Commission were themselves later accused of high treason (so much for 'live rats'), only Norfolk escaped violent death because the King died of syphilis. Only Richard Rich – the real 'rat' perhaps – prospered and died peacefully. So did the Common Man, because he kept himself out of trouble – and his advice to the audience (implicating them again) is that they should do the same.

Act 2, scene 6

Summary

More has been imprisoned for a year. The Jailer wakes him at one in the morning to take him before the seventh Commission (Cromwell, Norfolk, Cranmer, with Rich and the Jailer as witnesses) to attempt to make him swear to the Act of Succession. More will recognise the offspring of Queen Anne Boleyn as heirs, because the King in Parliament told him that they are; but he will not swear to the Act, and he will not say why. Norfolk 'assumes' the reasons for More's silence are treasonable; Cranmer 'guesses' his objectives. More protests that all they *know* is that he will not swear to the Act, and, in law, they cannot 'assume' or 'guess' anything further. Norfolk appeals to More to come with them 'for fellowship'. More refuses, and says he has no doubts about why he refuses to take the oath, but he will tell nobody but the King. Cromwell threatens him with 'harsher punishments'; More says he is not threatened by 'justice'. He asks for more books and to see his family; Cromwell refuses. When More has left, Cromwell makes the Jailer swear that he had never heard More mention the King's divorce or marriage and bribes him with fifty guineas. The Jailer wants 'no part of it'. Cromwell tells Rich to remove More's books, and says the King is impatient for an outcome. When Cranmer and Norfolk have left, Cromwell broods on using the rack, but decides the King would not permit it. Rich approaches Cromwell about the vacant post of Attorney General for Wales.

Commentary

Continuing the patterning of this play, a bell struck one (in the morning) when More was first questioned by Wolsey in the first Act. Although More has been in prison one year (which emerges later in the scene), he is *relaxed* because he knows, under the law, he is innocent. Norfolk, for friendship's sake, asks for a chair for More. (There is historical evidence that this happened.) More, politely thanks the Jailer. As soon as the official introduction is over, Norfolk calls More 'Thomas', still thinking of him as a friend.

More is in control of this interview, because he knows the law better than do his judges. Ironically Cromwell has to thank More for explaining the 'law' to Norfolk. More remains alert and clear-headed throughout, and there is never any doubt that he will not sign, or say why he will not. His exchanges with Cranmer and Cromwell are sharp and decisive.

Political and religious trials, where people are 'assumed' to be guilty because of the views they are 'thought' to hold, have been common in many countries in many ages. What Bolt is saying is that nothing can be 'assumed', 'supposed' or 'guessed' in law, and he speaks for all defenders of human rights when he says this.

The episode over More's books (for which, once again, there is historical evidence), gives the excuse to introduce Rich's eventual perjury in the final trial scene. This is Cromwell's 'gentler way' that he mentions to Rich at the very end of the scene, with the bribe of the position of Attorney-General of Wales.

The way that Cranmer makes the Jailer take the oath makes a mockery of the solemnity of oath-taking (as perceived by More), and this is further emphasised by Cromwell backing it up with a bribe of fifty guineas. This is too much even for the Jailer, who comes to the *decision*: 'I want no part of it.' (He is no Judas, taking fifty pieces of silver.)

The characters of Rich and Cromwell are well brought out at the end of this scene: Rich can think only of his advancement; and there is no doubt that Cromwell would have used the rack if it were not that he knew the King would not allow it.

Act 2, scene 7

Summary

The Jailer wakes More to say his family (Alice, Margaret and Roper) have come. After much restraint, Margaret admits they were allowed to come to try to persuade him to take the oath and come out of prison. More replies he would lose his 'self' if he took the oath; it was just because the state was evil, that people who would stand fast were needed. If he could find a way out, he would. He tells them to leave the country. More says he could 'make a good death' if he thought Alice understood why. She protests she doesn't understand, but, finally, says he's the best man she had ever met. More tells them to take half the food they had brought to Bishop Fisher (also imprisoned). They say their farewells, in spite of the Jailer.

Commentary

(Note: The first part of this scene is studied in detail on pages 75–81.) This is the final scene in the play where More is seen with his family, and the final test of his steadfastness, because his family could have been his biggest excuse not to 'stand fast'. Furthermore, it is Margaret, the daughter whom he loves and respects so much, who tempts him with three arguments. The first, that he should say the words of the oath and think otherwise in his heart, he answers by showing his integrity; he takes an oath with his whole self; and Margaret readily agrees. Her second argument is that by standing fast against a state that is three-quarters evil, he is electing himself a hero; but More answers this by saying that to remain human, and given the choice, he must stand fast and risk being a hero; and this wasn't a matter of reason, but of love. Margaret's third temptation is emotional – she briefly but graphically gives a picture of the misery of their home without him; but More dismisses this as mental torture.

More's answer to Margaret's second argument reveals the key place of Man in the 'chain of being'. Animals and angels do not have to choose between good and evil, but man does; and if a man is to remain human, he must choose to stand fast against evil; More says that the 'choice' is not made through reason, but through love, emotional rather than intellectual. This answer, although it lists the medieval seven deadly sins and opposes them to a mixture of classical and Christian virtues, is directed at the modern audience. Bolt is saying that it is 'common' (in any state in any age) for 'avarice, anger, envy, pride, sloth, lust and stupidity' to profit much more than 'humility, chastity, fortitude, justice and thought'; so good men, at any time, to remain human, must 'stand fast'.

The entrance of the Jailer, allowing them two minutes, makes these last few moments even more tense. But even here, to gain a moment or two extra, More will not stoop to bribery; but the way he gets round it shows how far he is prepared to go – gambling and drink. Even here, More shows he is in control and thorough. He knows this is the last time he will see his family, and he has prepared for the moment. There are two things he must do: save them by getting them abroad; and make his peace with Alice. The first they agree to, but the second is most difficult for More. That he loves Alice is not in doubt, but he doesn't know how best to approach her. His flattery of her custards and dress, quite justifiably, is rebuked. Notice the stage directions in this important exchange: he regards her *with frozen attention*; *he nods once or twice*; *holds out his hands*; but she refuses them, *remaining where she is, glaring at him; he is in great fear of her* and *just hanging on to his self-possession*. When she tells him, frankly and honestly, that she doesn't understand why he has to die, *she throws it straight at his head*, which leaves him *gasping*. But then, *swiftly she crosses the stage to him*; *he turns and they clasp each other fiercely*. Their actions speak with more force than their words. But, once Alice has given in, the warmth between them which has not been expressed before is sincere and moving.

Even at this moment, More thinks of others, asking Alice to take half the custard to Bishop Fisher.

The eruption of the Jailer onto the stage makes the possibility of dig-nified farewells impossible. Notice that *the heavy, deliberate bell continues, reducing what follows to a babble*. As so often in real life, the really moving moments are made chaotic by the intrusion of 'the common man', insensi-tive to others, but anxious for his 'position' and to keep himself out of 'trouble'. However, Alice throws him off, and does make her last exit *with considerable dignity* on the last stroke of the bell.

More's answer to the Jailer's last appeal that he was a 'plain simple man and just wanted to keep out of trouble', is meant by Bolt to be a passionate cry against all the 'plain simple men' – and women – who think only of themselves, 'to keep out of trouble'.

Transition

Summary
With much stage activity, with comments from Cromwell and the Common Man, the stage is set up as a court of law, with the Common Man as the Foreman of the jury.

Commentary
The intense stage activity generated at the end of the last scene is *immediately* intensified to introduce the last scene and climax of the play. In fact, there is so much activity, with the *music*, portentous and heraldic, and with all the panels with the royal monogram, and *an enormous Royal Coat of Arms*, that the effect is satirical and borders on farce: all these *trappings of justice* are needed to attempt to arraign More, who, meanwhile, sits humbly studying the scroll given him by the Jailer.

The satire is emphasised by the twelve folding stools made to represent the jury, with the 'hats' worn by the Common Man placed over them. Cromwell adds to the mock-heroic tone with his rhyming couplets. His role in this transition is purposely out of character. He shows himself to be another 'Common Man' who can stand aside and comment on the action. But he is an intelligent 'common man' who uses other common men for his own purposes. (Notice, later in this scene, that it is Cromwell who removes the Common Man's prop basket from the stage. After Cromwell has used him for his last role as Headsman, there are no more parts for the Common Man to play.) The exchanges between the Common Man, who is caught by Cromwell as he attempts to tiptoe discreetly off the stage, and is then made to actively demonstrate the pun of the 'cap fitting', add to the satirical tone.

But there is also a more sinister undercurrent embedded in the farce. The *large hour-glass* that the Common Man places on the table is a clear indication that More's last hour has come. Cromwell's couplets also contain significant puns: the 'Rigging of the Law' is not only the Ship's rigging; and Cromwell himself is going to 'fix' the Law in more senses than one. Furthermore, the jury is rigged by 'wire-pulling', the Common Man 'fixing' the wires, and Cromwell 'fixing' the Common Man, as he does at the end of the 'trial' in the next scene.

So, by a complex combination of farce, satire, mock splendour, puns and quibbles, all with a sinister undertone, the audience is prepared for the mockery -- and the 'splendour' of More's performance -- of the last scene.

Act 2, scene 8

Summary

More appears before Cromwell, Norfolk and Cranmer at the Hall of Westminster on a charge of high treason. The Common Man is the Foreman of the jury. Norfolk opens by telling More that the King would pardon him if he would repent. More replies that his petition is to God to keep him in his honest mind. He says he is weak and asks to sit – which Norfolk allows.

Cromwell opens the charge by letting slip the information that More's friend, Bishop Fisher, had been executed that morning. The charge is that More denied King Henry his title of 'Supreme Head of the Church in England'. More says his silence was not denial. When reminded by Norfolk that the charge was now high treason, for which the punishment was death, More says death comes to us all. When More said he stood upon his silence, Cromwell gives his reasons why More's silence was 'a most eloquent denial'. More replies that, in law, 'silence gives consent', and the Court must construe according to the Law. The Loyal subject must be loyal to his conscience out of respect for his soul, which More equates with a man's 'self'.

Cromwell calls in Rich who swears that when removing More's books, he had heard More say that Parliament had not the competence to make King Henry Head of the Church. More says he is sorrier for Rich's perjury than his own peril, and when he asks for the witnesses, he is told they are away in Ireland, but had left their depositions. More realises he is 'a dead man' and deals ironically with Rich. The 'jury' find More guilty.

More now, having 'fulfilled all his obligations', speaks his mind that the Act of Supremacy was repugnant to the Law of God, but it was because he would not accept the marriage that Cromwell sought his blood. He is condemned to be beheaded, and the Common Man is made executioner by Cromwell. On the way to the scaffold, Norfolk offers More drink, Margaret 'flings herself upon' her father and he says his farewell to her, and More deals brusquely with the Woman who said he gave false judgement. More tells the Headsman not to be afraid of his office, because he was sending him to God.

After the execution there are alternative endings: either (a) Cromwell and Chapuys join up self-mockingly as 'men who know what the world is and how to be comfortable in it'; or (b) the Common Man tells the audience that it's not difficult to keep alive if you don't make trouble.

Commentary

Norfolk, still feeling sympathy for More, has to *take refuge behind a rigorously official manner* because that is the only way he can hide what he really feels, and later he *leans forward urgently*, trying to make More save his own life. Cromwell, however, trying to unsettle More, approaches him from behind, and then, *informally* but quite purposely, lets slip the news that Bishop Fisher had been executed that morning.

When More's silence in refusing to take the oath is brought up again, More senses that the trial had been 'rigged', because he knows he had shown before, that, in law, he is safe. And he shows he is not afraid of death by his graphic description of how death comes to us all, even Kings, and he also includes all present in his phrase 'yours and mine', none of whom is worthy of an easy death when compared with Christ. (This fine speech is based on a passage from one of More's own works, *Dialogue of Comfort*, which is quoted by R. W. Chambers. See page 55.)

Cromwell's argument about More's silence being a 'most eloquent denial' of the King's supremacy, sounds persuasive, but More knows that in law, 'silence gives consent'. More's grasp of the law, and what it can do, is much firmer than Cromwell's; and when More moves on to 'matters of conscience', the two men are exposed as being at extremes of the moral spectrum, which is why they *hate each other and each other's viewpoint*.

More's viewpoint needs careful consideration. This is one of the key moments in the play. That he *earnestly addresses* the Foreman (who, as the Common Man, stands for us all) on the 'matters of Conscience', and then *turns back* to it, after being distracted, puts more dramatic emphasis on this important moment. He will not be distracted from making this point clear, and the audience's attention is caught by Bolt by the false start, and then the second beginning. 'The loyal subject is more bounden to be loyal *to* his conscience than to any other thing.' To More, this is 'very and pure necessity for respect of my own soul', which he then explains: 'A man's soul is his self!' Here he is not giving a Christian explanation of 'soul', but a humanist one. It is that part of any human being to which any individual is bound to be loyal if he is to remain human. In the Nüremberg Trials after the Second World War (1939–45), the Nazi war criminals argued that they were only carrying out orders of their superiors when they committed their atrocities; but the Court ruled that, as a human being, a person's first loyalty is to his own conscience.

This viewpoint is opposed to Cromwell's, to whom the state, King and country are all-important. We should remember Machiavelli, who was mentioned at the very beginning of the play; but even more, totalitarian states which are ruled by a dictator, and some politicians in democratic states, who suggest that a subject's first loyalty is to his country. More, who has shown himself to be a great patriot, is *not untouched* by Cromwell's mention of *'a great native country'*, but his reply is unanswerable: one cannot help one's country by being a liar, and being disloyal to one's own self'.

Cromwell immediately brings in a liar and perjurer. This is the only way he can 'fix' More, the 'gentler way' he had 'rigged' with Rich. It had been carefully organised and rehearsed, with the witnesses being conveniently absent. Rich, in the very first scene of the play, had said he wanted to be 'used' and to have some 'decent clothes'; now even Norfolk is impressed by his *dress and bearing*, and having learnt his lesson from Machiavelli, he amorally is prepared to be 'used' by Cromwell and perjure himself for the post of Attorney General of Wales, which Cromwell has at his disposal as a convenient bribe.

There are few stage directions in this passage; it doesn't need any because the exchanges are cold and clinical. Norfolk has two directions, *sharply* and *strung up*, because he finds it difficult to believe Rich's testimony. More *gestures helplessly* on the news that the witnesses cannot be called, because this is his final proof that the 'trial' had been rigged. Then More looks into Rich's face with *pain and amusement*; 'pain' because he feels pity for any man who can commit such perjury; 'amusement' because of the irony of giving your soul away for Wales, which at that time was regarded as a very primitive place. And notice he calls Rich by his first name, Richard; he thinks of the vulnerable young man he had been, and how he had been corrupted. But Rich exits *infrangibly dignified*; he is not going to have his hard-won dignity broken by any moral strictures.

Earlier, More had addressed Cromwell with another statement which recalls many political trials: 'What you have hunted me for is not my actions, but the thoughts of my heart. It is a long road you have opened. For first men will disclaim their hearts and presently they will have no hearts. God help the people whose Statesmen walk your road.' This applies, of course, to any country, at any time.

As soon as More has been found guilty, his manner changes. There is an important stage direction: *More has a sly smile. From this point to the end of the play his manner is of one who has fulfilled all his obligations and will now consult no interests but his own.* A man's 'obligations' have not been mentioned, as such, before; but the implication is that More's strict moral code had been ruled by his obligations to his King, country, family and friends. In an effort to save himself, these obligations had stopped him from saying and doing many things; as he says, 'To avoid this I have taken every path my winding wits could find.' But now that he knows he is 'a dead man', he can, at last, 'discharge his mind'. He has nothing to lose.

He first declares that the Act of Supremacy was illegal, because Parliament could not bestow Spiritual Supremacy; both Magna Carta, and the Coronation Oath affirmed that neither King nor Parliament could control the rights of the Church. He then, *very quietly* and *ruminatively*, gives his final thoughts. In both the radio and television plays he says the words that the historical More is reported to have said on the scaffold: 'I am the King's good servant; but God's first.' Here he echoes only the first half to show his loyalty to his country. But he cannot stop himself from the last *great flash of scorn and anger*: it was not really the Act of Supremacy that had caused his death, but because he would not agree to Henry's divorce from Catherine. 'I'll brook no opposition,' Henry had said, when he had earlier discussed this with More in the garden. And so it proved to be.

After the sentence of death, Bolt uses another great flurry of stage activity, involving flying machinery, dramatic lighting effects, crowd noises, which are all made *naturally* and *technically* to show, in metaphor, how the state deals with a dissident. It is efficient and impressive.

Cromwell then uses the Common Man for his last role, that of Executioner. We remember, ironically, that his first role had been More's Steward. After this, it is Cromwell who symbolically drags the props basket off stage, because the state had no further use for the Common Man in any further role. He had fulfilled his multi-purposes.

More, on his way to the scaffold, is met by four people who symbolise his previous 'obligations': Norfolk, who represents friendship, with whom he deals *quite coldly*; Margaret, representing the family, he speaks to *dispassionately*, after disengaging himself from her; the Woman, who represents his dealings with society, he dismisses *crisply*; and Cranmer, representing the Church, he speaks to *quite kindly*, but yet refuses his final blessing. More's only obligation is now to himself when he meets his God.

Bolt relies on stage machinery for his final climax, with the *harsh roar of kettledrums* and the *total blackout*. This is meant to shock the audience.

Both endings have a tone of cynical irony. In the first, the two men who were supposed to be enemies show that they recognise each other as cynical pragmatists, 'men of the world', who know how to exploit it for their own ends.

The alternative ending takes the irony and the cynicism more directly to the audience. The Common Man identifies himself with the members of the audience, who will 'recognise' him because each is just such a cowardly, time-saving common man. Although this pill is sugared with a coating of humour, the audience should taste something of its bitter medicine.

4 THE HISTORICAL SOURCES OF THE PLAY

4.1 BOLT'S HISTORICAL SOURCES

In his Preface, written in September 1960, Bolt tells us just about everything we need to know about 'the bit of English History which is the background to this play'. Further details, such as precise dates, are given by the Common Man in his transitional interludes between the scenes. So, with the Preface, and information gleaned from the scenes, the play is self-explanatory, even to anyone who knows nothing about English sixteenth-century history. However, a study of the historical sources, and how Bolt chose either to use them, or not to use them, or to adapt them, can tell us something about why he used this 'bit of English History'.

Bolt's chief source for the play seems to have been R. W. Chambers' *Thomas More*, first published in 1935. Bolt mentions this book in his interview with Ronald Hayman. Chambers uses all the previous biographies, and also the works, speeches and letters of More himself, and his book contains most – if not all – of the references and quotations that Bolt uses in the play. Interestingly enough, Chambers' biography is not divided into chapters, but has a Prologue, five Acts and an Epilogue, which might itself have suggested to Bolt that More's story could make a good play.

In the Prologue Chambers writes: 'This book attempts. . .to depict More not only as a martyr (which he was) but also as a great European statesman; More's far-sighted outlook was neglected amid the selfish despotisms of his age; yet his words, his acts, and his sufferings were consistently, throughout life, based upon principles which have survived him. More was killed, but these principles must, in the end, triumph. If they do not, the civilisation of Europe is doomed' (page 15). This, in itself, could have suggested to Bolt that More's life was significant for his own times.

He says in his Preface that he started on his play with 'some such ideas in mind that. . .we no longer have. . .any picture of individual Man. . .by which to recognise ourselves and against which to measure ourselves; we are anything. But if anything, then nothing, and it is not everyone who can live with that, though it is our true present position.' Against this 'centre which is empty', both socially and individually, Bolt sets what he calls More's 'adamantine sense of his own self'.

4.2   THE MAIN CHARACTERS

Furthermore, if this were not enough to suggest the subject of a play to Bolt, further on in his Prologue, Chambers writes: 'We have, then, four main characters – More and his wife, Roper and his wife – acting upon each other. Behind them we have the background of the world, the flesh, and Henry VIII. The world: represented by the Duke of Norfolk, scandalized, when he came to dine with More at Chelsea, to find him in church, singing in the choir, with a surplice on his back. Norfolk protested, as he went arm in arm with his host to the Great House, "God's body, God's body, my Lord Chancellor, a parish clerk, a parish clerk! You dishonour the King and his office." More replied, and certainly with truth, that King Henry would not consider the service of God a dishonour to his office.' (page 29). Here are *six* of the main characters of Bolt's play, and the suggestion of an excellent dramatic incident and piece of lively dialogue, which, indeed, Bolt used almost verbatim:

NORFOLK: Yes – d'you propose to meet the King disguised as a parish clerk? (*They fall upon him and drag the cassock over his head.*) A parish clerk, my lord Chancellor! You dishonour the King and his office!

MORE   (*appearing momentarily in the folds of the cassock*):   The service of God is not a dishonour to any office.

A further character is also suggested by Chambers in his Epilogue where he concludes that More 'is the consistent opponent of the new ideas which found literary expression in Machiavelli's *The Prince*, and were embodied in the person of Thomas Cromwell' (page 360). Chambers says that there is some evidence that Cromwell had read Machiavelli in manuscript. The Machiavellian theme, after being introduced in the very first scene, runs throughout the play as a counter to More's 'conscience'. The encounters between More and Cromwell, who at one time are said to 'hate each other', are amongst the highlights of the play. They embody not only the historical 'opponents', but also the modern conflict between the authoritatian power of the state and the rights and obligations of an individual's conscience.

Yet another main character is suggested by a historical incident at More's trial. Chambers records it thus:

> The case against More was not going well. What was wanted was not evidence of how he justified his silence, but evidence that he had broken it.
>
> Rich stepped forward.
>
> He asserted that in the Tower, on 12 June, More had uttered the fatal words to him. Rich had said to More, 'Admit that there were an Act of Parliament that all the realm should take me, Richard Rich, for King; would not you, Master More, take me for King?' 'That would I,' More had replied, 'but take a higher case; how if there were an Act of Parliament that God should not be God?' 'That cannot be,' Rich had replied. 'But I will put a middle case: you know that our King has been made Supreme Head. Why will you not take him as such, even as you would take me as King?'
>
> Then, Rich asserted, More had replied that, though a King could be made by Parliament, and by Parliament deposed, it was not so with the Head of the Church.
>
> More denied the conversation:
>
> 'If I were a man, my Lords, that did not regard an oath, I needed not, as it is well known, in this place, at this time, nor in this case, to stand here as an accused person. And if this oath of yours, Master Rich, be true, then pray I that I never see God in the face; which I would not say, were it otherwise, to win the whole world.' (pp 337–8)

Bolt develops this in two ways. He makes Rich one of the major characters of the play, as an 'example' (as in a medieval morality play) of how an ambitious young man who has 'no centre' can be 'used' and corrupted in his quest for riches and power, until he arrives at this final act of perjury. Secondly, Bolt uses much of the dialogue, slightly adapted, in the trial scene in the play; but he adds his own extra piece of wit to show More's contempt and pity for Rich. Rich's 'price' for this act of perjury was to be appointed Attorney-General for Wales by Cromwell; Bolt makes More's final comment to his 'old friend': 'Why, Richard, it profits a man nothing to give his soul for the whole world. . .But for Wales –!'

4.3 THE ADAPTATIONS

Robert Bolt did not research the life of Sir Thomas More in any academic sense. He didn't need to. He was not setting out to write an historical pageant, so strict accuracy of historical fact and quotation was not needed. However, in his introduction to his other play which is based on an historical subject, *Vivat! Vivat Regina!*, he writes:

> The writer of an historical play is a kind of playwright, not a kind of historian. But I think he is obliged to be as accurate, historically, as he can.
>
> He has borrowed not only his story but some of his emotion from actual people who actually lived. He is in debt to them for their virtues and vices, imaginatively energized by the actual energy they expended. He owes them the truth and is a kind of crook if he does not pay up.
>
> (Heinemann, 1971, p.vii)

Arthur Miller, in his 'Note on the Historical Accuracy' of his play *The Crucible* wrote: 'This play is not history in the sense in which the word is used by the academic historian.' Bolt could have written the same of his play. He had found the subject he wanted – the example of a man with an 'adamantine sense of his own self' to set, by implication, against modern man with his 'empty centre'. Then, keeping truthfully to the main outline of More's life, against a roughly accurate background, he adapted, selected and shaped to give the greatest theatrical impact – and modern point – to his play.

For example, More had four daughters, one son, and numerous grandchildren, but no mention is made of any of them in the play, apart from Margaret. It is historically true, as the letters testify, that Margaret was his favourite daughter, and that she was extremely clever and intelligent. She, as well as More himself, corresponded in Latin with Erasmus who was one of the most intellectual men in Europe. So Bolt achieves much greater theatrical impact by having all More's filial love concentrated on this one devoted daughter rather than having all the other children and grandchildren prancing around on the stage.

Another example of Bolt's adaptation is the dramatic importance he gives to the Duke of Norfolk, who, among other things, represents the theme of true friendship in the play. It is historically true that Norfolk was a friend of More; but Bolt makes Norfolk More's only true friend in the play, and then, ironically, makes him pronounce sentence on More.

This is not historically true, because although Norfolk was a member of the Commission, it was Lord Audeley who passed sentence and who also forgot to ask More if he had anything to say. But it is, dramatically, more effective to concentrate the action on Norfolk, and not diffuse it, so losing the irony, with another character. Similarly, there is some historical evidence that More was offered a cup of wine when he was on his way to the scaffold, to which he replied, as in the play: 'My master had easel and gall, not wine, given him to drink.' The person offering the goblet could have been his adopted daughter, Margaret Clement; but it certainly was not the Duke of Norfolk. However, in the play, the action serves as a symbol for the strength of true friendship.

4.4 THE MODERN SLANT

These examples are typical of the many small adaptations that Bolt makes. He was not, it must always be remembered, writing a historical pageant where every detail must be accurate; he was writing a play which uses a historical setting and characters to make a comment - by comparison and implication - on the way we live now. Very often, in fact, it is just these adaptations - what Bolt chooses to put in, and what to change or leave out - that give us an indication of what he is pointing to. For example, Bolt tends to play down More's frequent references to God as a Christian would understand that word; instead, he emphasises More's references to his 'conscience', and relates this to his sense of his 'self', which Bolt makes More equate with 'soul', using this last word in a way that would not be understood by many Christians. Some critics, Ronald Hayman for example, have jibbed at this, calling it historically inaccurate. But it is certainly true that More placed great emphasis on the importance of a man's conscience - which, by implication, gave him liberty over the rules of any king or state. As he said at his trial, as reported by Chambers: 'Ye must understand that, in things touching conscience, every true and good subject is more bound to have respect to his said conscience and to his soul than to any other thing in all the world beside' (pages 336-7; compare page 92 of the play). It is this tendency in More, which looked away from feudal times towards modern concepts of freedom of conscience, that Bolt brings out. A Catholic writing a religious play about More would perhaps emphasise the devotional side of More's character.

4.5 HISTORICAL AUTHENTICITY

There are many smaller incidents and comments in the play which are based on historical fact. For example, the incident when Margaret brings in a great heap of bracken, which some theatre critics thought was a bit far-fetched, is based on Harpsfield's *Life of More*, written a few years after More's death, but not published until 1932.

> Chambers records:
>
> How great More's poverty then was, we learn from Harpsfield:
>
>> "He. . . was enforced and compelled, for lack of other fuel, every night before he went to bed to cause a great burden of fern to be brought into his own chamber, and with the blaze thereof to warm himself, and his wife, and his children, and so without any other fires to go to their beds.
>
> We can imagine Mistress Alice More, shivering over the embers of a fire of Chelsea bracken, and reflecting that her husband had refused a sum which would have placed them all in luxury.   (page 32)

In fact Bolt used not only Harpsfield's *Life*, but also Chambers' suggestion about Mistress Alice, to make a telling dramatic moment.

The gift of £4,000 from the clergy, which More refused, is also historically true; as is Roper's spell as a Lutheran, although it is recorded that this was so after he married Margaret, and not before, as in the play. Another small adaptation of a recorded incident is that it was Bishop Fisher who sent More 'half a custard', and not the other way round, as in the play; although More sent many gifts (not mentioned in the play) in return. It would be easy for an historian to quibble about the historical accuracy of the play; but such criticisms would be missing the point.

There are, as well, many recorded phrases and sentences that Bolt uses to colour his play and give it a feeling of authenticity. Chambers quotes Harpsfield again as making Dame Alice ask her husband: 'What will you do, that you list not to put forth yourself as other folk do? Will you sit still by the fire, and make goslings in the ashes with a stick as children do?' (page 154). Historically, Dame Alice is supposed to have said this because of More's lack of ambition; in the play, she says it after More had resigned the Chancellorship. Later, More's comment: 'But at the worst, we could be beggars, and still keep company, and be merry together!' is taken from Chambers (page 284) where only the last nine words are quoted from Roper's *Life*. Even More's reference to Margaret as 'Eve' in the scene where she tries to persuade her father to come out of prison, is found in the *Letters*. And the very title of the play comes from one of the historical comments on More, written soon after his death by Robert Whittinton, and which are quoted by Chambers (page 177) and by Bolt himself (page xxvi). Some of More's most famous and telling words, spoken on the scaffold, 'I am the King's good servant, but God's first', Bolt sacrificed in the stage play, although they were the climax of the original radio play. The reason is probably that, on the stage, to have made More say anything so pithy at such a dramatic moment would have detracted from the impact of the actions, and Bolt, as a playright and writer of film scripts, knew that actions speak more powerfully than even such telling words.

4.6   THE SHAPE OF THE PLAY

The shape of Bolt's play could also have been suggested by Chambers, whose Act III begins with these words:

> For twelve years More served the King, before his career was crowned by his succeeding Wolsey in the Chancellorship. To all appearances, his life during these years was one of steadily increasing distinction and power. In reality, these years saw the hopes which More cherished for his country and for Christendom one after another overthrown. And, as each blow falls, we can see More's own destruction brought one stage nearer. The Chancellorship, which to the world may have looked like the culmination of a successful career, was in reality the last of many successive strokes of doom.
>
> Fortune's wheel was a medieval commonplace - all the time that men tied to it are rising to the summit, they are drawing nearer to the moment when the revolution of the wheel must plunge them down. (page 157)

Chambers' Act III is half-way through his biography; Bolt's Act II, that is half-way through his play, begins with More resigning the Chancellorship, which is the symbol of 'the moment when the revolution of the wheel must plunge him down'. The shape of the play is similar to that of *Macbeth*; in Shakespeare's play Macbeth's evil schemes prosper until exactly half-way through, when, with a short stage direction, *Fleance escapes*, in Act III, scene iii, his wheel of fortune turns. Bolt uses the same arched form, the apex coming exactly half-way through. But in Bolt's play there is also a mirror image of More's fall, and that is the rise of Richard Rich. As Ronald Hayman says: '*A Man for All Seasons* is a graph on which Bolt plots two curves: the steady rise of an opportunist and the decline of a man of principle.' This 'graph' is part of the essential irony of the play.

4.7 THE TONE AND STYLE

But apart from the plot, shape, characters and various incidents that were 'given' to Bolt by the historical facts, even more important is that the whole tone and style of the play were dictated by the tone and style of More's own life, speeches and writings. Chambers comments: 'More and Socrates are two of the greatest masters of irony who ever lived. . .More had a habit of uttering his deepest convictions in a humorous way, and his wildest jokes with a solemn countenance (page 18). This ironic contrast, as we have seen, is brought out in the shape of the play. It is also brought out in several scenes in the play which have a solemn or tragic subject, but which yet, on the stage, border on farce. A good example is the transition to the last scene, with all its flying props, portentous music, mock jury, and comic exchanges between Cromwell and the Common Man, all of which are used to introduce the scene that is to see More's trial and execution. Another example is the message that comes down to the Common Man in a large envelope during the transition scene before we see More in prison: all three members of the Commission were later accused of high treason, and only Richard Rich, the perjurer, prospered and died a peaceful death.

Finally, the style in which much of the play was written was determined by More's own prose style. In his Preface Bolt says: 'I was guaranteed some beauty and form by incorporating passages from Sir Thomas More himself. For the rest my concern was to match with these as best I could so that the theft should not be too obvious.' It is remarkable – perhaps a tribute to the remarkable nature of the man himself – that so many of More's words, in the form of his speeches, letters and books, have survived. His Complete Works, being published by Yale University, so far extend to fourteen volumes, and this does not include the many letters that have survived. His son-in-law, Roper, in his Life of Thomas More, which was written twenty years after More's death, also recalled many of the conversations he had heard in the More household. So Chambers, and Bolt, had plenty of examples of More's own words to draw on.

The chief area where Bolt used More's own words most faithfully was in the trial scene. Here is how Chambers records some of More's reactions, as reported by Harpsfield, after More had been found guilty:

After the verdict of 'Guilty' there was no way to escape. It was the sign for which More had been waiting, the sign that help would not fail him, and that now he should 'abide by his tackling'. . . . He interrupted Lord Audeley: 'My Lord, when I was toward the law, the manner in such a case was to ask the prisoner, before judgement, why judgement should not be given against him.'

Audeley stayed his judgement, and demanded what More had to say. He answered:

'Seeing that I see ye are determined to condemn me (God knoweth how) I will now in discharge of my conscience speak my mind plainly and freely touching my indictment and your Statute withal.

And forasmuch as this indictment is grounded upon an Act of Parliament directly repugnant to the laws of God and his holy Church, the supreme government of which, or of any part whereof, may no temporal prince presume by any law to take upon him, as rightfully belonging to the See of Rome, a spiritual pre-eminence by the mouth of our Saviour himself, personally present upon earth, only to St. Peter and his successors, bishops of the same see, by special prerogative granted; it is therefore in law, amongst Christian men insufficient to charge any Christian man."

. . .'We now plainly perceive that ye are maliciously bent'. said Norfolk.

'Nay,' replied More, 'very and pure necessity, for the discharge of my conscience, enforceth me to speak so much. Wherein I call and appeal to God, whose only sight pierceth into the very depth of man's heart, to be my witness. Howbeit, it is not for this Supremacy so much that ye seek my blood, as for that I would not condescend to the marriage.' (pages 340–1)

Compare these words with the words of the play (pages 96–7) and you have an excellent example of how Bolt quoted, adapted and condensed the original words, both to give historical authenticity to his play, and to bring out the modern parallels.

Another piece of adaptation is More's splendid speech on death that he delivers earlier in the trial scene (pages 90–1). This is adapted, not from one of More's speeches, but from one of his prose works, *Dialogue of Comfort*. Here is the original passage, as quoted by Chambers:

And therefore, but if he be a fool, he can never be without fear, that either on the morrow, or on the self-same day, the grisly, cruel hangman, Death, which, from his first coming in, hath ever hoved aloof, and looked toward him, and ever lain in await on him, shall amid all his royalty, and all his main strength, neither kneel before him, nor make him any reverence, nor with any good manners desire him to come forth; but rigorously and fiercely gripe him by the very breast, and make all his bones rattle, and so by long and divers sore torments, strike him stark dead, and then cause his body to be cast into the ground in a foul pit, there to rot and be eaten with the wretched worms of the earth, sending yet his soul out farther unto a more fearful judgment, whereof at his temporal death his success is uncertain.

Shortly afterwards, Chambers quotes another sentence, from the same work, which is also used by Bolt:

Who can for very shame desire to enter into the kingdom of Christ with ease, when himself entered not into his own without pain?

4.8 CONCLUSION

It must clearly be understood that this use of original sources, much of it via Chambers, in no way detracts from the originality of Bolt's play. Nobody would dispute the originality of Shakespeare's plays; but Shakespeare used his sources even more extensively than does Bolt. For example, G. B. Harrison says in his Introduction to the Penguin edition of *Troilus and Cresside*: 'In writing his Roman plays Shakespeare had used Sir Thomas North's translation of Plutarch's *Lives* and followed his source so closely that he adapted whole passages almost verbatim.' The same could be said, with, of course, different source material, of most of Shakespeare's plays. In fact, not one of Shakespeare's plays is set in his own times, not one of them has an original story, and most of the characters are 'borrowed' from previous sources. One thing that distinguishes Shakespeare's plays is the clear-sighted vision over why and how the original material is being used, and the brilliant adaptation and augmentation of the language to bring out the theme of each play, and make its greatest dramatic impact. All this is also true of Bolt's *A Man for All Seasons*. And just as Shakespeare's plays, because of their universal validity, are appreciated by world-wide audiences in all ages, so, I am sure, will Bolt's play be appreciated. It is, truly, A Play for All Seasons

5 THEMES

5.1 THE CONTEMPORARY SCENE

The historical background of *A Man for All Seasons* is to be found in the 1950s rather than in the sixteenth century. It was the time of the British invasion of Egypt; the Soviet invasion of Hungary; the time of the development of The Bomb in Britain, and the movement against it; the time of the heightening of the Cold War between the 'West' and Russia, between the 'Free World' and Communism. In Britain, a key word of the decade was 'committed', and one group of 'committed' writers published their 'beliefs' in a book, typically called *Declaration* (Tom Maschler (ed.) MacGibbon & Kee, 1957). Here is how one of those writers, Doris Lessing, saw the 1950s:

> We are living at a time which is so dangerous, violent, explosive and precarious that it is a question whether soon there will be people left alive to write books and to read them. It is a question of life and death for all of us; and we are haunted, all of us, by the threat that even if some madman does not destroy us all, our children may be born deformed or mad. We are living at one of the great turning-points of history. In the last two decades man has made an advance as revolutionary as when he first got off his belly and stood upright ...And because of this, the great dream and the great nightmare of centuries of human thought have taken flesh and walk beside us all, day and night. Artists are the traditional interpreters of dreams and

nightmares, and this is no time to turn our backs on our chosen responsibilities, which is what we should be doing if we refused to share in the deep anxieties, terrors and hopes of human beings everywhere. (page 16)

But it was a time of a battle of beliefs rather than – for most of the world – of bullets and bombs. The 1950s was a time when everyone, particularly artists, the 'unacknowledged legislators of the world', had to declare their allegiance. In the 'West', they had to be for their own country and against Communism, and vice versa: there was no third alternative. This formula is applied by both Chapuys and Cromwell to More in Bolt's play. It is also used by Arthur Miller in his play written during the 1950s, *The Crucible*: 'A person is either with this court or he must be counted against it, there is no road between.'

One of the most typical manifestations of the 1950s was the revival of the Un-American Activities Committee in the United States, which was in session when Bolt was writing *A Man for All Seasons*. But a play which this Committee affected even more, and one which is similar to Bolt's play in many ways, was Arthur Miller's *The Crucible*.

5.2 A PARALLEL WITH ARTHUR MILLER'S *THE CRUCIBLE*

One of the tasks of the Un-American Activities Committee was to search for 'subversives' in the entertainment industry in the United States. The Communist Party had been declared a 'conspiracy', so anyone who had shown leftish tendencies was under suspicion. As a young man, Miller, like Bolt, had been attracted to Marxism, and continued to be left of centre. He had taken part in various festivals and movements which were deemed to be 'communist inspired'. He was called before the Committee and asked questions not only about his own past, but also about other people he had associated with. This he refused to do, and his reason was very close to More's reason to refuse to answer: 'I am trying to and I will protect my sense of myself. I could not use the name of another person and bring trouble on him.' (Benjamin Nelson, *Arthur Miller: Portrait of a Playwright* (Peter Owen: London, 1970)). After a long hearing, Miller 'refused to repent' and was at first sentenced to the maximum penalty of $1,000 and one year in jail; but this was later reduced and then quashed on a legal appeal. But Miller, and Bolt, had seen the dangers of this mass nationalistic hysteria. Even before *The Crucible* was first produced in the

United States, Miller had said in an interview, published in the *New York Herald Tribune* on January 25th, 1953:

> ...nobody wants to be a hero. You go through life giving up parts of yourself - a hope, a dream, an ambition, a belief, a liking, a piece of self-respect. But in every man there is something he cannot give up and still remain himself - a core, an identity, a thing that is summed up for him by the sound of his own name on his own ears. If he gives that up, he becomes a different man, not himself. (Nelson, page 169)

Arthur Miller wrote *The Crucible* in the early 1950s, before he became embroiled in the machinations of the Committee of Un-American Activities in 1956, but he was fully aware of the prevailing political climate when he was working on the play. Interestingly enough, Bolt also wrote his play a few years before he was imprisoned for his part in the Committee of One Hundred (see page 5). Both playwrights had anticipated, if not deliberately embraced, their own futures.

Miller also chose a historical setting for his play, but this setting, as he said, is the play's 'occasion rather than its subject'. When asked why he had never written another historical play, Miller replied: 'I didn't do it again I suppose because I never thought of another period that was so relevant to ours. . .' (Ronald Hayman, *Arthur Miller* (Heinemann: London, 1970)).

The Crucible tells the story of mass hysteria in Salem, Massachusetts in the seventeenth century, with its resulting witch-hunt. Miller saw the parallel with the corporate national hysteria in the 1950s in America against left-wing 'subversives'. In the Introduction to his *Collected Plays* (Secker & Warburg: London, 1955), Miller explores this parallel, and he concludes:

> Above all, above all horrors, I saw accepted the notion that conscience was no longer a private matter but one of state administration. I saw men handing conscience to other men and thanking other men for the opportunity of doing so.

Against this mass hysteria and the abrogation of the obligations of the individual, Miller puts one brave man, Proctor, who - as was said of Miller by the chairman of the Un-American Activities Committee - 'refuses to repent'. And Proctor, like More, dies for it.

5.3   THE INDIVIDUAL AND THE STATE

As can be seen, the main theme of *The Crucible* is very close to that of *A Man for All Seasons*: the conflict between an individual's conscience and the demands of state administration. *The Crucible* was first produced in Britain in November, 1954, at the Bristol Old Vic, only four months after the first radio version of *A Man for All Seasons* was broadcast. Bolt saw this early production of Miller's play. It is quite usual for artists to work on the same theme at the same time; dominant themes are 'in the air', expressed by the pressures of the times. Furthermore, between the first radio version of Bolt's play, broadcast on 26th July, 1954, the television version in January, 1957, and the stage version of July, 1960, the issues were more clearly defined by subsequent political events, and also, on a personal level, by what was happening to Miller in the USA, and also to Bolt himself with his involvement in the Ban the Bomb campaign.

In his Preface to *A Man for All Seasons*, written in September, 1960, Bolt explains why he chose More as the hero of his play. He begins with 'our present position':

> We no longer have. . .any picture of individual Man. . .by which to recognise ourselves and against which to measure ourselves; we are anything. But if anything, then nothing, and it is not everyone who can live with that, though it is our true present position.   (page xi)

During the troubled times of the 1950s, when beliefs were being questioned, it was natural for 'committed' artists to ask themselves: 'What are my obligations as a human being?' Miller and Bolt answered this question in a similar way: a man's final obligation is to his own 'self', that part of him that makes him human: Miller used the words 'identity' and 'core'; Bolt used the words 'self' and 'soul'; and both used the word 'conscience'. This is why Bolt chose More as his hero:

> Thomas More, as I wrote about him, became for me a man with an adamantine sense of his own self. He knew where he began and left off, what area of himself he could yield to the encroachments of his enemies, and what to the encroachments of those he loved. . .At length he was asked to retreat from that final area where he located his self. And there this supple, humorous, unassuming and sophisticated person set like metal, was overtaken by an absolutely primitive rigour, and could no more be budged than a cliff.   (page xii)

5.4   THE RADIO PLAY

The radio version of the play, which Bolt wrote first, is much more straight-forward in its theme and treatment than the stage version which he wrote about six years later. Its main theme is the clash between the individual conscience and the state, embodied in the clash between More and King Henry. It has as its climax the famous words, recorded as having been spoken by More on the scaffold: 'I die the King's good servant, but God's first.' In the television version of the play, the viewers are spared the sight of the scaffold on their screens, but More speaks these words to the 'Lieutenant' in his cell before he goes out of a door into 'incandescent sunlight' to his execution. But these words which are the epitome of the conflict between the individual conscience and the state were omitted from the stage version. The theme of the conflict that arises between a man of conscience and his family is in both the radio and television plays, embodied in the two characters of Dame Alice and Margaret. The conflict with friends is also in both plays, embodied in the person of Norfolk, but it is not so well developed into a theme of what constitutes true 'friendship'. In the radio play, Margaret says of Norfolk: 'He – he begs your forgiveness, Father, but (*Her voice trembles*) – he dare not be seen with you.' And, at the very end of the play, it is an anonymous 'Lieutenant' and not Norfolk who offers More the drink when he is on his way to the scaffold. The Machiavellian theme is only hinted at: in the radio play, Cromwell, who has a much smaller part, is described as 'a man who believes in doing what "must be done"'. In the television play, this is slightly developed by More saying of Cromwell: 'He is a man of action by principle. I mean he believes in "doing what must be done".' But there is no mention of Machiavelli. The inadequacy of 'principles', as embodied by Roper in the stage play, is not in the radio or television plays, in which Roper is not one of the characters; but there is a suggestion in More's comment on Cromwell. But the greatest change between the two earlier versions and the stage play is the development of the theme of the individual's 'self'. More's speech: 'But there's a little...little, area...where I must rule myself', and his speech to Meg in the Tower where he cups his hands and says, 'if he opens his fingers *then* – he needn't hope to find himself again', are not even hinted at in the earlier plays. One wonders if some of Miller's words suggested to Bolt the relevance of this theme at a time when so many people were having to 'make a stand'. When it came to Bolt himself having to define his own 'true present position', he realised he could do this only by finding his own 'self'. He couldn't live with 'being nothing', but had to explore 'where he began and left off, what area of himself he could yield to the encroachments of his enemies, and what to the encroachments of those he loved'.

5.5 THE 'SELF' AND ITS COUNTER-THEME

What, then, is this play about? Bolt himself said, 'It is not easy to know what a play is "about"' (page xii). It is particularly difficult when a play is as elaborately patterned as is this play, with all its themes interwoven, and where nearly every theme has its opposite mirror-image.

The main theme is the importance of a man having a sense of his own 'self', that 'area of himself' which makes him the man he is, and which he cannot yield to anyone, neither his enemies nor those he loves. If he is to be anything, he must keep this part of himself inviolate; otherwise he is 'nothing'. Bolt makes More equate 'self' with 'soul' when he says to Cromwell, 'A man's soul is his self!' But the word 'soul' here, although used historically by More as a devout Christian, is used by Bolt as a metaphor for 'self'. To More, a man is judged when his soul (or 'self') stands 'before his Maker'; to Bolt, a humanist and non-Christian, a man must judge himself, and the concept of 'going before one's Maker' remains a metaphor. More tries to make Norfolk find this 'area of himself' when he says: 'Is there no single sinew in the midst of this that serves no appetite of Norfolk's but is, just, Norfolk?' (page 73). The 'self' is not a physical part of the body. More's 'adamantine sense of his own self' still survives.

The counter-theme to the sense of 'self' is embodied in the play by the Common Man and Richard Rich. The Common Man starts by being More's Steward and ends by being his executioner, being willing to play any part that came his way. This is Bolt's way of saying that 'our true present position', that of the common man, is to be 'anything. But if anything, then nothing'. It was a brilliant stroke by Bolt to coalesce all the small parts of the radio and television plays, of Narrator, First and Second Boatmen, Gaoler, Jurymen, Executioner, etc., played by different actors, into a multiple part played by one actor, the Common Man, who thus enacts, with his symbolic 'props basket', the very embodiment of a man with no sense of his own 'self', but is 'anything', and so, because he can at no point make a 'stand', is led to be the executioner of his master. It was also a brilliant stroke to bring Rich into the very beginning of the stage play, where, in both radio and television plays, he appears only at the very end with the perjured 'evidence' against More. In the stage play, he provides, right from the beginning, the mirror-image of More. He has no sense of his own self, but is willing to be 'used' by anybody in order to advance his own materialistic ambitions.

5.6 CONSCIENCE VERSUS MACHIAVELLI

Closely associated with the theme of 'self' is that of 'conscience', which is counterbalanced by the Machiavellian theme. In the radio and television plays, this is the main theme – the individual conscience pitted against the power of the state, embodied by More and King Henry, and encapsulated in More's words: 'I am the King's good servant, but God's first.' In all three versions of the play, More's words spoken to Wolsey are almost unchanged; 'I believe, when statesmen forsake their own private conscience for the sake of their public duties. . .they lead their country by a short route to chaos' (page 12). But in the stage play, it is only a man who has a sense of his own 'self' (or 'soul') who can be loyal to, or reject, his conscience. Cromwell tells Rich: 'You're not a man of conscience.' He can't be because he has no 'self'. The crucial conflict takes place in the trial scene, between Cromwell and More:

MORE (*Earnestly addressing him*): In matters of conscience –
CROMWELL (*bitterly smiling*): The conscience, the conscience. . .
MORE (turning): The word is not familiar to you?
CROMWELL: By God, too familiar! I am very used to hear it in the mouths of criminals!
MORE: I am used to hear bad men misuse the name of God, yet God exists. (*Turning back to jury*.) In matters of conscience, the loyal subject is more bounden to be loyal *to* his conscience than to any other thing.
CROMWELL (*breathing hard: straight at* MORE): – And so provide a noble motive for his frivolous self-conceit!
MORE (earnestly): It is not so, Master Cromwell – very and pure necessity for respect of my own soul.
CROMWELL: – Your own self you mean!
MORE: Yes, a man's soul is his self!

Cromwell, interestingly enough, is a man with a sense of his own self, but he rejects any loyalty to his own conscience because his spur for action is not Christian or humanist, but Machiavellian. As More says of him in the television play: 'He is a man of action by principle. I mean he believes in "doing what must be done".' And 'what must be done' is for the benefit of the state; the individual's conscience has no part in the equation. And that Cromwell is a Machiavellian is made clear at the very beginning of the stage play, when Rich tells More that it was Cromwell who had recommended him to read 'Signor Machiavelli'. And as with 'soul', 'Machiavelli' is also used as a metaphor by Bolt, to stand for all those people and forces that consider the interests of the state (or country, or 'security') overrule the individual conscience.

5.7 INTEGRITY, HONESTY AND LOYALTY VERSUS CORRUPTION AND BETRAYAL

Clustered around these two interrelated themes of 'self' and 'conscience' – with their counterparts – are a group of other interrelated themes: integrity, honesty and loyalty, as against corruption and betrayal. More's honesty is never in doubt: as Norfolk says of him: 'Goddammit he was the only judge since Cato who *didn't* take bribes' (page 58). Neither is his loyalty to his country: Norfolk again: 'Crank he may be, traitor he is not' (page 58). Neither will he betray anyone else: 'I have no window to look into another man's conscience. I condemn no one (page 78). Against this are opposed the corruption of Wolsey and Rich, against whose final dishonesty and perjury More does not wish to survive. There is also the cowardly betrayal of the Common Man (as Steward, Boatman and Jailer) summed up in the words: 'I'm a plain simple man and just want to keep out of trouble', to which More cries out passionately: 'Oh, Sweet Jesus! These plain simple men!' And even the otherwise loyal Margaret is made to be disloyal to her father's trust in her, and her trust in him, by taking an oath to try to persuade him to swear to the Act of Succession.

5.8 THE LAW

Related to these themes is that of Law. More's respect for the law, rather than 'what's right', is expounded at length to Roper and Margaret when they try to make him have Rich arrested: 'This country's planted thick with laws from coast to coast - Man's laws, not God's - and if you cut them down - and you're just the man to do it - d'you really think you could stand upright in the winds that would blow then?' (page 39). His trust in the law is also shown by his defence of himself: 'Qui tacet consentire. . .Silence Gives Consent (page 92). This is broken only by Rich's blatant perjury, engineered by Cromwell, who has no respect for law: 'It's just a matter of finding the right law. Or making one (page 61).

5.9 THE FAMILY

All these interwoven themes, which are universal, not confined to any time or place, are played out against a background which provides other inter-related and universal themes. The love and loyalty within the family is given great prominence in the play, concentrated in the love and trust between More and his daughter Margaret, but also brought out in More's final scene with Alice: 'I understand you're the best man that I ever met or am likely to (page 86). There is also More's trust of Roper, in spite of his 'principles': 'Will, I'd trust *you* with my life. But not your principles (page 41). And one reason why More wanted to reject Norfolk as a friend, when he realised Norfolk himself was threatened, was because 'you have a son'. Against this, Wolsey, Rich and Cromwell have no family, as far as the play is concerned; and King Henry rejects his wives to suit his own aims.

5.10 FRIENDSHIP

Love within the family is closely related to love of friends, and true friend-ship is embodied in the play in the person of Norfolk: 'I'm fond of you, and there it is! You're fond of me, and there it is!' (page 71). This is explored at great length throughout the stage play, culminating in Norfolk offering More the goblet of wine when he is on his way to the scaffold. In both radio and television versions, this is done by an anonymous Lieutenant. Against this 'true friendship' is placed the use that Rich makes of his 'old friends'. 'Friends', to Rich, are people to be 'used', or who will make use of him, so long as he gains something from it. In fact, the phrase 'We're old friends', used many times in the play, has a cynical ring to it.

5.11 POWER

Finally, there is the theme of state power, embodied in King Henry, as opposed to all the transcendental values such as conscience, friendship, love, and so on. Bolt has said that he used a poetic image for this theme:

'As a figure for the superhuman context I took the largest, most alien, least formulated thing I know, the sea and water. . . Society by contrast figures as dry land' (page xvi). This theme, and how it is treated by this poetic image, is explored in Section 6.

5.12 CONCLUSION

One of the best summaries I know of the meaning of this play is con-contained, incidentally, in *An Approach to Shakespeare* by L. C. Knights. This summary shows that the main theme of *A Man for All Seasons* is relevant to all times and places, no matter what the religion or politics of the protagonists. Professor Knights is writing about Boethius, whom he describes as being 'one of the main transmitters of pagan philosophy to the Middle Ages'. His book, *De Consolatione Philosophiae*, which Sir Thomas More most probably knew, was written in prison when Boethius was awaiting death in AD 534. L. C. Knights writes: '*De Consolatione Philosophiae* of Boethius. . .is a sustained and varied demonstration of how man may find and preserve his essential nature under the impact of great adversity and great pertubation. At the heart of it is the perception that man's essential nature cannot be satisfied by anything less than the goodness which is the desired health of the soul: being, blessedness of virtue, and happiness are one and the same.'

6 TECHNICAL FEATURES

6.1 DEVELOPMENT FROM THE RADIO PLAY

A Man for All Seasons was not originally written as a stage play. It was first written as a radio play, and first broadcast by the BBC in July 1954. It was immediately successful and was given a second radio production. Bolt then wrote a shorter television version of the play, lasting only one hour, which was first transmitted by the BBC on New Year's Day, 1957. These earlier versions had their effect on the technique he adopted for the stage play.

In a radio play the action flows on from one scene to the next with no interruption. All changes of scene must be conveyed to the audience either verbally or by other sounds. Often minor characters are used to indicate where each new scene is taking place. In his radio play, Bolt used a large number of minor characters – a Boy, Secretary, First and Second Boatmen, Steward, Clerk, Dicon (More's servant), Juryman, Gaoler and Executioner – played by different actors, to move the action swiftly from one scene to the next.

In the television play, which textually is very close to the radio version, scene changes could be indicated visually but most of the minor characters, played by different actors, were included to maintain the flow from one scene to the next. But in neither the radio nor the television version do any of these useful minor characters have any real impact on the action of the drama. They are really technical devices to 'place' the action and keep it moving.

There is one place where one of the minor characters, the Gaoler (or Jailer as he becomes in the stage play), interacts with More himself, and

a comparison of the three versions gives an example of how the play
developed. Here is More in the Tower in the radio play:

GAOLER: Still writing, Sir Thomas? You'll gravel yourself, that's what
you'll do. Here's a currant pie from the Lord Bishop, with his thanks
for the custard.

MORE: How is he?

GAOLER: Pretty fair, sir. He's a game old bird. He's to be tried tomorrow
by the New Act.

MORE (*Startled*): For denying the King's Supremacy? He has denied it?

GAOLER (*With conscious diplomacy*): Well, sir. (*Whispering*) He said to
ask you to pray for him and to tell you to 'beware of trickery'.

MORE: He has not denied it, then?

GAOLER: I don't know, sir. I forget now just what he said.

MORE (*Sighing*): Ah, well. Thank you for what you remembered.

GAOLER (*Virtuously*): I'm a plain, simple man myself, sir; it's best for
me not to meddle in these things.

MORE: Sometimes I think there's nothing worse can happen to a country
than to have plenty of plain, simple men in it. But thank you for
your message.

GAOLER: That's all right, sir. Goodnight. You understand my position,
don't you, sir?

MORE: Yes, I understand your position. Goodnight.
The cell door closes. Music.
Fade in the Duke of Norfolk's voice

NORFOLK: (*Speaks loudly, very much in his official capacity*): . . .are
called before us here at the Hall of Westminster to answer charges of
high treason. . .

In the television play, in the scene where Alice and Margaret visit Thomas
in the Tower – Roper does not appear at all in either the radio or television
plays – when Alice pleads for more time, this reaction follows:

GAOLER: I'm a plain simple man, my lady.

MORE (*Passionately*): Oh sweet Jesus, you plain simple men!

The action then goes directly to the Courtroom.
In the stage play, the 'plain simple man' comment is again directed at
More, after Alice has left:

MORE: For God's sake, man, we're saying good-bye!

JAILER: You don't know what you're asking, sir. You don't know how you're watched.

ALICE: Filthy, stinking, gutter-bred turnkey!

JAILER: Call me what you like, ma'am; you've got to go.

ALICE: I'll see you suffer for this!

JAILER: You're doing your husband no good!

MORE: Alice, good-bye, my love!

> *On this, the last stroke of seven sounds,* ALICE *raises her hand, turns, and with considerable dignity, exits.* JAILER *stops at head of stairs and addresses* MORE, *who, still crouching, turns from him, facing audience.*

JAILER (*reasonable*): You understand my position, sir, there's nothing I can do; I'm a plain simple man and just want to keep out of trouble.

MORE (cries out passionately): Oh, Sweet Jesus! These plain, simple, men!

> *Immediately:*   *(1) Music, portentous and heraldic.*
>   *(2) Bars, rack and cage flown swiftly upwards.*
>   *(3) Lighting changes from cold grey to warm yellow, re-creating a warm interior.*
>   *(4) Several narrow panels, scarlet and bearing the monogram 'HR VIII' in gold are lowered. Also an enormous Royal Coat of Arms which hangs above the table stage right.*
>   *(5) The* JAILER, *doffing costume comes down the stairs and. . .*

Then follows the 'rigging' of the jury, which consists of the different 'hats' worn by the Common Man, with the props basket remaining clearly visible on the stage, before we go into the Court Scene.

6.2 THE USE OF THE COMMON MAN

Several important developments that affected the technique of the stage play took place between the radio version of 1954 and the stage version of 1960. The first was the stroke of genius to amalgamate all the minor parts into the Common Man, who then plays all the other minor characters. He is there, in embryo, with his multiple facets, in the radio play; but it was not until Bolt had developed the concept of 'self' in the stage play, that the Common Man, playing so many roles, was born as the ironic reversal of More's consistent self-hood. The Common Man, as a character used to implicate the audience, could have been born from More's passionate cry in the television play, 'Oh sweet Jesus, you plain simple men!' But he is already implicit in the stage direction, *Virtuously*, in the radio play. Bolt is already getting at the 'virtuous' plain, simple men of his radio audience. So, in the stage play, the 'props basket' becomes the symbol of the Common Man's willingness to play any part, so long as he can 'keep out of trouble'.

And, of course, as soon as the Common Man had been invented, he became the link man between the scenes, which flow from one to the other as they do in the radio and television versions. He is also the link between the play and the audience, moving in and out of the action on the stage, making a connection between the historical setting and the relevance of the action for 'all seasons'. As he says at the very beginning of the play: 'The Sixteenth Century is the Century of the Common Man...Like all other centuries.'

Some critics have called the Common Man a Brechtian 'alienating' device, making the audience aware that they were watching actors performing, so they can isolate themselves from the action on the stage. Bolt does use the Common Man to link the scenes as Bertolt Brecht, the German playwright (1898-1956), uses some of his characters, but far from 'alienating' the audience, Bolt uses the Common Man to draw the audience into the action. Bolt wants to implicate the audience. One thing he is saying in the play is that it is you, the 'plain simple men' in the audience, who allow things like this to happen, and to feel 'virtuous' about it. This is why the alternative ending to the play finishes with the Common Man addressing the audience:

> I'm breathing...Are you breathing too?...It's nice isn't it? It isn't difficult to keep alive friends...just don't make trouble – or if you must make trouble, make the sort of trouble that's expected. Well, I don't need to tell you that. Good night. If we should bump into one another, recognise me.

Of course we should recognise him: he is our cowardly, virtuous selves – unless we happen to be saints.

6.3 THE USE OF STAGE MACHINERY

The second technical development between the radio and stage versions of the play is Bolt's increased awareness of the possibilities of modern stage machinery. His second stage play, *Flowering Cherry*, first performed in London in 1957, enabled Bolt to become intimately involved in the possibilities of the modern stage, with its sophisticated technology for sound, lighting, flying props, and all the other effects. He was excited by these possibilities, and used them to the full. Some comments which he makes about his later historical play, *Vivat! Vivat Regina!*, apply equally to *A Man for All Seasons*: 'I had to adopt a form of play which could leap across both miles and months without a break, without a change of set; an overtly theatrical, highly artificial form. I happen to like that kind of play. . .' (page xi). And later, in a 'Note to the Designer', he says: 'My intention is to maintain a smoothly continuous narrative to which changes of time and place will seem incidental. . .' and that 'the lighting, not the properties, will create the changes of time and place, and mood' (page xxv). In *A Man for All Seasons* use is made of a few symbolic props, such as the 'envelope' that 'descends swiftly' to the Common Man, and the 'rack' and the 'cage'; but, generally, the set is the same throughout, the table and chairs are multi-purposed, and the changes of place and mood are made by 'varied lightings', as Bolt says in his note on the set. It was, perhaps, the technical possibilities of professional stage lighting, the department that is usually so inadequate on the amateur stage where he had previously operated, that most excited Bolt. Lighting effects are used extensively, not only to create changes of place and mood, but also to enhance the imagery of the play, when, for example, More is left 'isolated in the light' (page 66), or when the 'rear of the stage becomes water patterned' (page 69).

But there is one place in the play where the whole flurry of technical activity makes a symbolic comment. The action after the word *immediately* in the stage directions from the stage version given on page 69, is really a demonstration of stage technique, used purposely as a metaphor for all the portentous apparatus of the State being brought against an individual dissenting voice. Bolt obviously enjoyed this great flurry of activity, showing just what the stage machinery can do. But the flurry has meaning within the play as satirical comment, which is then followed by the flurry of satirical puns and quibbles about 'rigging' and 'fixing' and the 'cap fitting' between the Common Man and Cromwell before the trial scene gets under way with Norfolk using almost the same words as in the original radio play. But the levels of sophistication and meaning have increased considerably.

6.4 THE USE OF LANGUAGE

The play has also become more sophisticated through the increased development of the careful patterning of the language. There are constant quibbles and puns and phrases repeated in ironic contrast. For example, 'We're old friends' is repeated in many circumstances, but always in ironic contrast to the true friendship as embodied between More and Norfolk. Both Chapuys and Cromwell, on different sides of the fence, use the same formula about More – if he is for us, he can't be against us: there is no third alternative. And there are many other repeated phrases, all contributing to the tight patterning of the play. One of the most telling examples is Norfolk's use, in the trial scene, of the words, 'Your life lies in your own hands, Thomas, as it always has', when we remember More's cupping of his hands when he was explaining his own 'self' to Margaret. Having gone over the ground twice before, when he came to write the stage play, Bolt knew his material intimately, and added new levels of meaning. It was as if, with the radio play, Bolt had started with a very pregnant theme, and then developed variations on it.

This verbal virtuosity, like the technical virtuosity, is directly related to the theme of the play. What increasingly struck Bolt about More was the ironic quality of the man and his life, and Bolt wanted to embody this irony within his play. In his Introduction to *Vivat! Vivat Regina!* he says: 'The playwright has a latent love for the play *form*, which he hopes will crystallize about his subject; he has in his heart a play-shaped vacancy which he will fill now with his subject' (page viii). And the form that crystallised about Sir Thomas More was one which gave almost endless possibilities for irony. Thus the play falls into two parts, shaped like an arc, with More's earthly rise and fall; and to embody the ironic contrast to this, in the stage play Bolt introduces Rich at the very beginning and shows his earthly rise. The Common Man is also, by his contrast changes of identity, an ironic counterpart to More, the final irony, of course, being that he starts as More's servant and ends as his executioner. But King Henry, with his illegal desire to put away Catherine and marry Anne, is, as the embodiment of the state, the main ironic contrast to More's steadfastness. At the very end of the trial More says, with a great flash of scorn and anger, 'Nevertheless, it is not for the Supremacy that you have sought my blood – but because I would not bend to the marriage!' (page 97).

6.5 THE USE OF IMAGERY

This conflict between More and Henry is enriched in the stage play by a whole new level of metaphorical meanings written in to the play. Bolt says in his Preface:

> In the play I used for this theme a poetic image. As a figure for the superhuman context I took the largest, most alien, least formulated thing I know, the sea and water. The references to ships, rivers, currents, tides, navigation, and so on, are all used for this purpose. Society by contrast figures as dry land. I set out with no very well formed idea of the kind of play it was to be, except it was not to be naturalistic. The possibility of using imagery, that is of using metaphors not decoratively but with an intention, was a side effect of that. . .If, as I think, a play is more like a poem than a straight narration, still less a demonstration or lecture, then imagery ought to be important. It's perhaps necessary to add that by a poem I mean something tough and precise, not something dreamy. (page xvi)

Within the play there are dozens of images relating to water, such as 'tides', 'currents', 'harbours', 'ships', etc. There are fewer images relating to the land, such as 'embankment', 'causeway', 'road', 'thickets', 'forester', etc., but the solid land is there by implication, being eroded by the illegal acts of Henry and Cromwell. More's defence of the law which he gives to Roper (page 39) is rich with contrasting water/land images. There are also a few highly significant images, such as 'mud' and 'quicksands', that are a mixture of land and water. It is Henry, who is 'eroding' society by illegally divorcing Catherine, who is said by Wolsey to be playing 'in the mud'. And when he comes to visit More's house he says, 'I happened to be on the river', and holds out his shoe proudly, saying, 'Look, mud'. In the film version Bolt takes this even further by having Henry jump from his royal barge, with obvious satisfaction, into several inches of mud, through which he then wades to the firm dry land of More's garden, itself an image of land cultivated and planted by man. And Cromwell, before the 'rigged' trial begins, mixes land and water in his couplet:

> So, now we'll apply the good, plain sailor's art,
> And fix these quicksands on the Law's plain chart! (page 89)

The word 'fix' is, of course, ambiguous, being used also in the sense that something is 'rigged', or arranged in a fraudulent way. And 'quicksands' is a most potent image because quicksands are places which look firm, but being a mixture of sand and water, are places where unsuspecting travellers flounder and are swallowed up – as, indeed, More was to be in the 'quicksands' that Cromwell had arranged with Rich.

Joseph R. McElrath, Jr, in an excellent essay on 'The Metamorphic

Structure of *A Man for All Seasons*', first published in *Modern Drama*, May, 1971, quotes from an interview that Bolt had with Charles Marowitz: 'Highly conventional theatre, where both sides of the footlights understand thoroughly what is going on, is like a drum-skin which is very, very tight. You tap it and it's resonant.' McElrath then goes on: 'It is a "resonance" that Bolt achieves in *A Man for All Seasons*. Each metaphorical sequence, reflecting figuratively the actions of the play, sounds its own note and echoes in unison with the others, stating and restating the theme. It is a "bold and beautiful verbal architecture" [which Bolt in his Preface says he tried to make] that Robert Bolt creates; and if his metaphor may be extended, the acoustics are perfect.'

7 EXAMINATION OF A SPECIMEN PASSAGE

In many literature examinations you can be given a long passage from your set book for detailed study. This is not the same as the much shorter context question where you are asked to say where the words come from, who said them, what came before and after, and, perhaps, asked to give the meaning of one or two words or phrases. With the longer passage, you are sometimes given some guidelines, such as: 'Write a detailed critical analysis of the following passage, relating it to the themes, style and characterisation'; or 'Comment on the meaning, imagery, tone and style of the following passage.' Whatever the instructions, read them very carefully, and make sure you answer every part of the question. In the first question above, for example, the marks would probably be equally divided between the three aspects – themes, style and characterisation; so if you commented on only one of the three, you would restrict yourself to one third of the marks. This is quite justified, because you have answered only one third of the question.

Having read the instructions to the question carefully, the next thing to do is to read the whole passage carefully, not just once, but two or three times even though you might know the passage quite well, and where it comes in the play. And with a play, as we have seen in the scene-by-scene commentary, you must read and consider the stage directions as carefully as the words spoken by the characters.

You must try to imagine how the action would appear on the stage. Look out, too, for changes in tone and feeling. With music, changes of speed, tone, loudness, etc., are written in by the composer, so the performer knows when the piece should be fast or slow, loud or soft. Such detailed instructions are not usually given by a playwright, although, as we have seen, Bolt does very often give full stage directions on how the actors should speak the words, and the actions they should perform. Bolt also gives stage directions to indicate dress and stage props. In this play, as well, he gives detailed instructions for the lighting plot, because Bolt realised, from his first experience of the professional stage, how much the lighting effects can add to the mood of various scenes. So, when commenting on a passage from the play, you must be aware of, and comment on, all the theatrical devices that are used in the scene.

Unless you are asked to do otherwise, do not spend too much time giving the plot of the play either before or after the scene. But you can, very briefly, give the context – that is, where the scene occurs in the play – in one short sentence.

Here is a typical passage that could be set, with a commentary on it:

Write a detailed critical appreciation of the following passage, relating it to the themes of the play:

> *From night it becomes morning, cold grey light from off the grey water. And enter* JAILER *and* MARGARET.
>
> JAILER: Wake up, Sir Thomas! Your family's here!
>
> MORE (*starting up. A great cry*): Margaret! What's this? You can visit me? (*Thrusts arm through cage.*) Meg. Meg. (*She goes to him. Then horrified.*) For God's sake, Meg. they've not put *you* in here?
>
> JAILER (*reassuring*): No-o-o, sir. Just a visit; a short one.
>
> MORE (*excited*): Jailer, jailer, let me out of this.
>
> JAILER (*stolid*): Yes, sir, I'm allowed to let you out.
>
> MORE: Thank you. (*Goes to door of cage, gabbling while* JAILER *unlocks it.*) Thank you, thank you. (*Comes out. He and she regard each other; then she drops a curtsey.*)
>
> MARGARET: Good morning, Father.
>
> MORE (*ecstatic, wraps her to him*): Oh, good morning – Good morning. (*Enter* ALICE, *supported by* WILL. *She, like* MORE, *has aged and is poorly dressed.*) Good morning, Alice. Good morning, Will.
>
>   ROPER *is staring at the rack in horror.* ALICE *approaches* MORE *and peers at him technically.*
>
> ALICE (*almost accusatory*): Husband, how do you do?
>
> MORE (*smiling over* MARGARET): As well as needs by, Alice. Very happy now. Will?
>
> ROPER: This is an awful place!
>
> MORE: Except it's keeping me from you, my dears, it's not so bad. Remarkably like any other place.
>
> ALICE (*looks up critically*): It drips!

MORE: Yes. Too near the river. (ALICE *goes apart and sits, her face bitter.*)

MARGARET (*disengages from him, takes basket from her mother*): We've brought you some things. (*Shows him. There is constraint between them.*) Some cheese...

MORE: Cheese.

MARGARET: And a custard...

MORE: A custard!

MARGARET: And, these other things... (*She doesn't look at him.*)

ROPER: And a bottle of wine. (*Offering it.*)

MORE: Oh. (*Mischievous.*) Is it good, son Roper?

ROPER: I don't know, sir.

MORE (*looks at them, puzzled*): Well.

ROPER: Sir, come out! Swear to the Act! Take the oath and come out!

MORE: Is this why they let you come?

ROPER: Yes...Meg's under oath to persuade you.

MORE (*coldly*): That was silly, Meg. How did you come to do that?

MARGARET: I wanted to!

MORE: You wanted me to swear to the Act of Succession?

MARGARET: 'God more regards the thoughts of the heart than the words of the mouth' or so you've always told me.

MORE: Yes.

MARGARET: Then say the words of the oath and in your heart think otherwise.

MORE: What is an oath then but words we say to God?

MARGARET: That's very neat.

MORE: Do you mean it isn't true?

MARGARET: No, it's true.

MORE: Then it's a poor argument to call it 'neat', Meg. When a man takes an oath, Meg, he's holding his own self in his own hands. Like water (*cups hands*) and if he opens his fingers *then* - he needn't hope to find himself again. Some men aren't capable of this, but I'd be loathe to think your father one of them.

Commentary

This passage is taken from the scene where More's family visit him in the Tower shortly before his trial and execution.

The tone of the scene is set by the 'cold grey light from off the grey water'; it is not a joyous dawn scene, but damp and cold. The 'cage' and the 'rack', at which Roper 'stares in horror', also add to the grimness of the background. More, confined like an animal, 'thrusts his arms through the cage'. This, we remember, is the only occasion that More's family were allowed to visit him in the Tower, so we see how 'awful' the place is through their eyes. Because both More and Alice have 'aged' since we last saw them, and because they are both 'poorly dressed', this adds to the depressing background. We are far removed from the lively and happy scenes in the Mores' family home earlier in the play.

Against this depressing setting, there is More's 'great cry' of surprise, and his 'ecstatic' joy at seeing his favourite daughter. More's initial confusion after 'starting up' is shown by his exclamations and short questions, but he quickly gets his wits about him when he is 'horrified' by the thought that Meg had been put in the Tower too.

Against this emotional family meeting, the Jailer plays a matter-of-fact, 'stolid' part. His drawn-out 'No-o-o', in spite of the stage direction 're-assuring', gives a hint that the Jailer knows why Meg has been let in, as does his comment that the visit is 'just a short one' – just long enough for Meg to tempt her father. Certainly his admission 'I'm allowed to let you out' indicates that he is under instructions. More, however, is still polite enough to thank the Jailer, but his 'gabbling' shows that, in his excitement, he is not completely in control of himself.

The first real indication that this visit is a put-up affair is when Margaret 'drops a curtsey'. If she had been completely at ease about this visit to her beloved father, she would have thrown herself upon him – as she does later in the play when More is on his way to execution. More, however, is 'ecstatic' to see his favourite daughter, so, when Alice enters, he has to smile at her 'over Margaret', whom he is still embracing.

That Alice enters 'supported by Will' evokes some sympathy for her. But whereas Margaret, through her love for her father (and, perhaps, her sense of shame, as we shall see later) doesn't seem to notice the conditions in the cell, Roper is horrified by the place. Alice's reaction is far from 'ecstatic': she peers at her husband 'technically' and addresses him 'almost accusatory', because she still thinks it is all his fault that he is imprisoned and they are all suffering for it. Her cryptic 'It drips' is her matter-of-fact, critical comment on the place. (The significance of the 'water' references within the metaphor that extends throughout the play is commented on in a later paragraph.) Notice that there is no physical contact between Alice and More; she is critical and cold and 'goes apart and sits, her face bitter'. 'Technically' is an odd word to use for the way Alice peers at More; perhaps Bolt means that because the light is not bright, and Alice's eyesight is no longer good, she has to 'peer' at her husband to see him clearly. Alice then 'goes apart' and takes no further part in this passage (although she makes her peace with More at the end of the scene), 'bitter' because of the suffering her husband's obstinacy is causing them all.

When Margaret takes the basket from her mother and shows her father the contents, an element of farce enters into the scene. Here they are with their last few minutes with their loved ones, and they talk of cheese and custard (the traditional dish of slap-stick comedy). But the 'constraint between them' causes Margaret to break down with the rather weak 'And, these other things. . .' because her sense of guilt about why she has come means she dare not meet her father face to face. More's enthusiastic repetition of her words 'Cheese' and 'A custard!' are meant to humour and encourage her, and when Roper, coming in for Margaret when she has broken down, offers the bottle of wine, More still has the consideration for others to ask, 'mischievously', exactly the same question as he had asked Roper about a bottle of wine at the beginning of the play (which reminds the audience of that happier occasion). It is only when Roper also breaks down with his weak response 'I don't know, sir' that More becomes 'puzzled' and looks at them. Why are they not able to make a better show of this special occasion?

More's 'Well' is the key turning point in the scene. It must be a very difficult word for an actor to pitch correctly. Notice that it does not have a question mark after it, so it is not a question. Neither does Bolt give any stage direction on how this key word should be uttered. It must convey More's realisation that all is not as it seems; this is not an innocent, straightforward visit by his family. Bolt leaves this crucial word to the judgement of the actor. It is like a modulation in music into a different and distant key.

Roper immediately blurts out the reason for their visit with his three short exclamations, and More immediately realises the truth; and when Roper admits that Meg was under oath to persuade her father to come out, More's voice changes from the 'mischievous' and 'puzzled' to 'cold'. Now we realise the reason for Meg's 'constraint': although she says she wanted to come to persuade her father to come out, she knew that he would see this as a lack of faith and trust in him, and an act of betrayal. In her heart, Meg knows that she will not be able to persuade her father to come out; but she would have liked to have the arguments to persuade him, and she is under oath to try. But Margaret is here at her weakest and most vulnerable – not really worthy, momentarily, of the great trust her father has in her. Although she quotes his own words at her father, she knows well enough that More would never say one thing and mean another; such hypocrisy is completely contrary to her father's character. To More, an oath is spoken directly to God, a commitment of his 'self' (or 'soul'), that part of himself that he must keep intact if he is to remain human. So Margaret's weak quibble on the word 'neat' (which is out of character and shows that her real 'self' is not behind her attempts to persuade her father) is promptly dismissed by her father with a deserved rebuke.

More then comes to the enactment of what taking an oath means to him. This is one of the key speeches in the play. The repetition of 'own' emphasises that each man is responsible for his own integrity. Nobody else is responsible – certainly not any state or king, and not even God. A person's *own* self is in his *own* hands'. Then the cupping of the hands and the image of the water shows just how vulnerable that 'self' is. We all know, from personal experience, how difficult it is to hold water in our hands, to stop it trickling through our fingers. So the cupping of the hands makes the audience (and Margaret) feel the preciousness of More's 'self'; it is his 'self' which is there cupped in his hands. It is a critical moment for a man's integrity, and this is stressed by the emphasis on the word *then*. If a man fails himself *then*, by opening his fingers (and the audience can so easily imagine the water escaping), he has lost his integrity as a human being for ever. This is true for any place or time for any person who believes in the integrity of each human individual. More acknowledges that not all men are capable of this difficult preservation of the 'self', but his 'I'd be loathe to think your father one of them' is an assertion of faith in his own self, and a rebuke to Margaret for her (temporary) lack of trust in him.

The 'water' image, although powerful on its own, is even more meaningful within the extended metaphor of water – including the river and the sea – as used throughout the play. Bolt says, in his own Preface to the play, that he used the image of water 'as a figure for the superhuman context'. So what More is holding in his cupped hands is the 'superhuman' part of himself, his 'soul' he calls it in one scene, that part of him which aspires towards the angels (which were made by God, More says elsewhere, 'to show his splendour').

But this is not the only 'water' image in the passage. When the stage direction says the cold grey light comes 'from off the grey water', it is saying, within the metaphor, that there is some 'superhuman' element in this scene, even though (or, perhaps, even *because*) More's body is in what Roper calls 'an awful place'. And when Alice says, critically, 'It drips!', she is saying, within the metaphor, that the place, in effect, stinks of foolish idealism (as she sees More's stand). So when More replies 'Yes. Too near the river', he is saying that the situation is too transcendental for her common sense practicality to understand.

It is doubtful if any member of an audience, seeing the play for the first time, is aware, even subconsciously, of the significance of these images. But it is one of the pleasures of studying such a finely wrought play as this, that these deeper meanings do become apparent, and they add to the power of the play. They show, as well, that Bolt himself was fully aware of the deeper implications of his play, which helps to give the whole drama, and its individual scenes, such a unified intensity.

8 CRITICAL RECEPTION

1   Mr Bolt resists all temptations to invent theatrical effects that would be foreign to More's gentle, lowly and affable temperament, but he provides Mr Paul Scofield with plenty of material out of which he makes a fascinating picture of a man who has always the intellectual measure of his opponents, who takes a serene delight in answering fools according to their folly and who is grave only when considering his duty as he conceives God sees it. No touch of priggish self-righteousness mars Mr Scofield's portrait of one whose mind in matters of social and political discussion has far outrun the range of his contemporaries and whose conscience will not let him take the easy way out of the deadly difficulties to which his popularity no less than his political capacity has exposed him. It is a portrait necessarily painted in low colours but appealing with quiet insistence to the imagination.

(From an anonymous review in *The Times*, 2nd July, 1960.)

2   Robert Bolt, who wrote *Flowering Cherry*, is not the first dramatist to take a play out of the long drawn resistance and final martyrdom of Sir Thomas More. Others have perhaps made the attempt on a richer theatrical swell of emotion. But that is not the way with Mr Bolt, who checks emotion with the fashionable tricks of a comic chorus master-cum-scene-shifter who plays many minor parts, winks at the audience, and in the current cant, "alienates" the drama for us.

(From a review by Philip Hope-Wallace in *The Guardian*, 4th July, 1960.)

3   *A Man for All Seasons*. . .has the attractions of a chase combined with the revelation of character of an unwilling martyr. It is both a police story and a tale of heroism. Mr Bolt himself has a mind fine enough to rise to

the occasions, and he writes in a style which avoids pedantry on the one
hand and vulgarity on the other.

(From a review by Harold Hobson in the *Sunday Times*, 3rd July, 1960.)

4   In *A Man for All Seasons* Robert Bolt has chopped the later career of
Sir Thomas More into a series of short and pithy episodes, each of which is
prefaced by a few words of comment and explanation addressed directly
to the audience. Changes of scene are indicated emblematically, by signs
being lowered from the flies, and the style throughout inclines to argument
rather than to emotional appeal. There is no mistaking whose influence has
been at work on Mr Bolt; the play is clearly his attempt to do for More
what Brecht did for Galileo.

In both cases the theme is persecution, and the author's purpose is to
demonstrate how authority enforces its claims on the individual conscience. More was a victim of the Reformation; Galileo, a century later,
fell foul of the Counter-Reformation; and both men, being contented
denizens of our planet, were extremely reluctant to embrace martyrdom.
Each found himself the servant of two masters. Galileo had to choose
between science and the Pope, More between the Pope and the King; each
of them, after years of hair-splitting and procrastination, ended up by
choosing the Pope – Galileo because he feared for his body, More because
he feared for his soul. According to Brecht, Galileo was disloyal to the new
science, and is therefore to be rebuked; according to Mr Bolt, More was
loyal to the old religion, and is therefore to be applauded.

I have no idea whether Mr Bolt is a religious man, but I am perfectly
sure that if someone presented him with irrefutable evidence that every
tenet of Catholicism was a palpable falsehood, his admiration for More
would not be diminished in the smallest degree, nor would he feel tempted
to alter a word of the text. The play's strongest scenes, all of which occur
in the second half, are those in which More, employing every resource of
his canny legal brain, patiently reminds his inquisitors that silence is not
to be equated with treason, and that no court can compel him to reveal
or defend his private convictions. His position, in short, is that he takes
no position; and I have no doubt that we are meant to draw an analogy
between More and those witnesses who appear before the Un-American
Activities Committee and take the Fifth Amendment.

(From a review by Kenneth Tynan in *the Observer*, 10th July, 1960.)

5   In *A Man for All Seasons* Robert Bolt has written a play that is luminous
with intelligence and steely with conviction. . .The theme of the play is
the pressure that a community of friends and foes brings to bear on a

man who can do no other but listen to the still, small voice of his conscience.

A *Man for All Seasons* is written with distinction. It combines in equal measure the dancing, ironic wit of detachment and the steady blue flame of commitment. With its commingling of literary grace, intellectual subtlety and human simplicity, it challenges the mind, and, in the end, touches the heart. For it is not only about a man for all seasons but also about aspirations for all time.

(From a review by Howard Taubman in the *New York Times*, 23rd November, 1961.)

6   *A 'Man for All Seasons' Implicates All of Us*

In *A Man for All Seasons* Robert Bolt has confronted a large, universal theme and coped with it humanly and grandly.

With poignancy and bitterness, wisdom and nobility he has restated fundamental truths that each generation must face. Although they are painful as well as glowing truths, they are communicated with so much grace of spirit and keenness of intellect that they not only stimulate but also exalt. . .The play. . .catches revelations pertinent for any age, including ours. . .

In *A Man for All Seasons* Mr Bolt brings many gifts to a theatre. To his powers of observation, his human sympathies and moral fervour he adds the indispensable talent – a flair for the stage. Using the flexible form of the chronicle play and the difficult device of a chorus, he has composed a work that cries out for theatrical expression.

(From a special article by Howard Traubman in the *New York Times*, 3rd December, 1961.)

7   More than four centuries after he was beheaded, a man of conscience has become the most impressive character of our theatrical season.

(From an article by Brooks Atkinson in the *New York Times* 15th December, 1961.)

REVISION QUESTIONS

1. Compare the characters and roles in the play of Sir Thomas More and Richard Rich.

2. Discuss the role of the Common Man in *A Man for All Seasons*, and say how you think the playwright expects the audience to react to him.

3. 'A Man for All Seasons...has the attractions of a chase combined with the revelation of character of an unwilling martyr. It is both a police story and a tale of heroism.' Discuss.

4. Explore the main themes in *A Man for All Seasons* giving close references to characters and incidents.

5. What problems of language did this historical play present to Robert Bolt, and how well do you think he dealt with them?

6. 'So far as style is concerned, the play is not particularly noteworthy. There is no great regard for words, or any unusual technique in their handling.' Do you agree with this assessment? Give detailed examples to support your views.

7. Soon after the play was first produced in America, a headline in the *New York Times* read: 'A "Man for All Seasons" Implicates All of Us'. Explore fully what the writer of this headline meant.

8. Write on the character of *two* of the following: Margaret, Alice, Cromwell, Roper, Norfolk.

9. *A Man for All Seasons* 'challenges the mind, and, in the end, touches the heart'. Do you agree?

10. 'To his powers of observation, his human sympathies and moral fervour he adds the indispensable talent - a flair for the stage. ' Discuss this assessment of Robert Bolt as revealed by *A Man for All Seasons*.

11. Explore fully how Bolt uses imagery in this play.

12. Why do you consider that *A Man for All Seasons* has been such a successful play in many different parts of the world?

FURTHER READING

Other plays by Robert Bolt

Flowering Cherry	1958
The Tiger and the Horse	1961
Gentle Jack	1964
The Thwarting of Baron Bolligrew	1966
Vivat! Vivat Regina!	1971
State of Revolution	1978

All these plays are published by Heinemann Educational Books and all have Prefaces written by Bolt himself.

Historical Background

R. W. Chambers, *Thomas More* (Cape, 1935). Now also available as a paperback, published by The Harvester Press Limited, 1982.

Alistair Fox, *Thomas More, History and Providence* (Basil Blackwell: Oxford, 1982).

Elizabeth Frances, (ed.) *The Correspondence of Sir Thomas More* Rogers, Princeton University Press, 1947.

The Yale Edition of *The Complete Works of Sir Thomas More*, Yale University Press. Fourteen volumes have so far been published.

Articles in journals

Anselm Atkins, 'Robert Bolt: "Self, Shadow and the Theatre of Recognition"', *Modern Drama* X, 1967.

Joseph R. McElrath, Jr, 'The Metamorphic Structure of *A Man for All Seasons*', *Modern Drama*, May, 1971. This interesting essay is reprinted in *Coles Notes*, 1982.

Biography

Ronald Hayman, *Robert Bolt*, Heinemann, 1969.